"I'm a woman who needs a God-sized miracle in a family situation. Linda's book gave me all of the tools for asking, waiting, and receiving extraordinary answers to prayer—not always in the way I was expecting—but with life-changing, trans-formational results. Read this book and you will agree that miracles still happen."

—**Carol Kent,** speaker and author of *Between a Rock and a Grace Place*

"If you've ever questioned if miracles exist today, once you've read this 'documen-tary' on Linda's life and those of reputable people who can prove that miracles are factual, you will no longer have doubts. In fact, you might be able to document the everyday miracles in your life. Linda even gives us assurance and encouragement when the miracles we want and pray for don't happen. This practical, easy-to-read, in-depth book eases our fears about miracles, shows us how to ask and expect miracles, and strengthens our faith as we wait for them to happen. Don't miss the opportunity to be informed, refreshed, and inspired by this book of sweet refuge into a life of realizing that miracles (not magic) happen in our lives."

—**Thelma Wells,** DD (Hon), president of a Woman of God Ministries and an AWSA Lifetime Achievement Award winner

Praise for Linda Evans Shepherd

"[Linda] does not share pat answers, she shares truth that will transform your life."

—**LeAnn Thieman,** coauthor, *Chicken Soup for the Christian Woman's Soul* and *Chicken Soup for the Christian Soul 2*

"Navigating through life's tough places, holding on to hope in the face of hopeless-ness, searching for purposes in our lives through the dialogue of prayer—this is the theme and gift Linda offers. Read and be encouraged through Linda's highly personal and powerful insight. She teaches us to fearlessly hold tight to the lifeline of powerful, practical interaction with our God."

—**Bonnie Keen,** author, speaker, recording artist

"In her new book, Linda reminds us that we can still expect miracles, we can still hear God's voice, and our prayers really make a difference. With so many diluted versions of the gospel around today, it is refreshing to see such genuine faith. Thank you, Linda."

—**Shirley Rose,** author; cohost, Aspiring Women Television

Other Books by Linda Evans Shepherd

When You Don't Know What to Pray: How to
Talk to God about Anything
When You Can't Find God: How to Ignite
the Power of His Presence
The Potluck Club Cookbook

NOVELS

The Potluck Club
The Potluck Club—Trouble's Brewing
The Potluck Club—Takes the Cake
The Secret's in the Sauce
A Taste of Fame
Bake until Golden

When You Need a Miracle

How *to* Ask God *for the* Impossible

Linda Evans Shepherd

Revell

a division of Baker Publishing Group
Grand Rapids, Michigan

© 2012 by Linda Evans Shepherd

Published by Revell
a division of Baker Publishing Group
P.O. Box 6287, Grand Rapids, MI 49516-6287
www.revellbooks.com

Printed in the United States of America

Library of Congress Cataloging-in-Publication Data
Shepherd, Linda E., 1957–
     When you need a miracle : how to ask God for the impossible / Linda Evans
     Shepherd.
          p.   cm.
     Includes bibliographical references (p.   ).
     ISBN 978-0-8007-2108-4 (pbk.)
     1. Prayer—Christianity. 2. Miracles. 3. Miracles—Biblical teaching. I. Title.
BV220.S54 2012
248.3′2—dc23   2012004796

12   13   14   15   16   17   18   7 6 5 4 3 2 1

For my brother, Jimmy, and his wonderful wife, Mary,
and their children, J.T. and Elizabeth

"I thank my God always
concerning you for the grace of God
which was given to you by Christ Jesus."
(1 Cor. 1:4 NKJV)

Contents

Foreword

Some twenty-first-century folks seem to think that miracles ended when the canon of the Bible was closed. Yes, they believe that in the Bible a donkey really did talk, a sea really got parted, Jews walked across on dry ground in search of the Promised Land, Jairus's daughter was raised from the dead, and Jesus ascended into heaven right in front of his followers. I agree that all those things actually happened. What I don't agree with is the contention that God is *not* in the miracle business today.

In Linda Evans Shepherd's new book, *When You Need a Miracle: How to Ask God for the Impossible*, she drives this point home with forthrightness and refreshingly transparent honesty. Her illustrations are relevant and encouraging.

Any book that begins with the promise "If you read this book until the end, you will experience miracles" had better deliver, and this one does. Linda speaks with the depth of experience of one who has needed miracles in her life. She asks, "How are we ever going to learn to walk on water if an occasional toilet doesn't overflow?"

But the takeaway from *When You Need a Miracle* isn't just that the author overcame setbacks and even, some would say, tragedies. It's a primer on seeking a miracle from God.

And like many things, it's almost as important to know what does *not* work as what does. One of the things I like most about this book is that it pulls no punches about the reason bad things happen in the first place. Linda is very frank about trying to get God to "perform" for us. Many tried to get Jesus to do amazing things when he walked the earth, just to see a miracle. It's not that God is stingy with his miracles. I think he's prudent. He's God. Indeed, God says no to our prayers when it serves his divine purpose.

Should we be so surprised that miracles are happening all around us? In the Gospel of John, chapter 14, Jesus told his followers immediately before his arrest and crucifixion that they would perform miracles even greater than he performed while he was here. That's an utterly astounding statement to a bunch of fellows who had walked with him for over three years and seen him make the lame walk and the blind see, calm a churning sea, turn water into wine, and make Lazarus come dancing out of a tomb when Jesus said, "Lazarus, come forth!"

And now he's telling them, his followers, and, I submit, those who believe today, that greater miracles would happen through us *after* he went to heaven! As in the here and now!

One of the excellent aspects of *When You Need a Miracle* is Linda's use of prayers and Scripture to ponder at the end of each chapter. She doesn't just give you discourse; you get practical, powerful prayers and God's Word to help you on your journey to the miraculous.

Linda ever so eloquently writes about what I personally experienced. I was killed in a car crash over twenty years ago. People who heard of my accident but not my death prayed desperately for me; one man even prayed over my dead body. God answered those prayers affirmatively, bringing me back to earth from the very gates of heaven. My head and chest were crushed in the head-on collision. I was told I would never walk again or have the use of my arm. Thirty-four operations, thirteen months in a hospital bed, and years of rehabilitation later, I am alive, walking and typing at this very moment with both of my hands. It is unequivocally because God is still in the miracle business that I live and function at all! Linda Evans Shepherd's book *When You Need a Miracle* explains how miracles come to be in the here and now.

Truly, I believe that God is doing some of his best stuff now! I've stood in too many hospital hallways and heard doctors remark incredulously, "We've done this test several times. We can't find the tumor now! It's just gone!" I've seen too many broken relationships restored, personal and/or financial catastrophes overcome. I have spoken to hundreds of congregations and other groups. At one such occasion, I met parents whose son clung to life in a nearby hospital. This was the first time they had left him. They came to hear a message of hope that night from a man who had experienced miracles. We prayed for their boy in the lobby of that church. Two years later at another speaking engagement, the same couple, faces beaming with delight, moved aside as they approached me to reveal their son walking and smiling, just like the doctors said he never would. Yes, I believe in miracles. I am one, and so was their precious son.

Linda offers this book with a timeless question and a remarkable promise: "Are miracles still possible?" and "If you read this book until the end, you will experience miracles."

I read it. I did. I was reminded that God is actively, intrinsically, lovingly involved in the world today.

Will you really take the time to look at his handiwork? God makes the impossible possible every day. Sometimes we just need something to remind us how to ask for it.

You're holding it in your hand.

Don Piper

Acknowledgments

How blessed I am to have my dear husband, Paul, our children, Laura and Jim, and my loving parents in my life.

I so appreciate my agent, Janet Kobobel Grant, and my editor, Vicki Crumpton, as well as all my wonderful friends at Baker Publishing Group.

I'm sending a special thanks to my friends and prayer partners, many of whom appear on the pages of this book: Carole Whang Schutter, Rebekah Montgomery, Joy Schneider, my Grace Bible study group, as well as the AWSA (Advanced Writers & Speakers Association) prayer team. How wonderful that God granted us miracles as we prayed together.

Thanks to all the wonderful people I've prayed with around the country. Your stories and answers to prayers inspired me.

Also, a special thanks to my readers. May God bless you as you discover his loving and miraculous ways, which include you.

It was a pleasure to write this book. I loved going deeper with God as I explored his magnificent prayer secrets.

1

Need a Miracle?

You are the God who performs miracles;
you display your power among the peoples.

Psalm 77:14

I'm guessing you picked up this book because you need a miracle. I've been there too, like the night, as a twenty-five-year-old newlywed, I came home from a weekend at the lake with my young husband and found a note taped to our apartment door: *Emergency! Call home.*

My husband carried in our bags while I rushed to the phone to call my mom. Her words tumbled through the thousands of miles of telephone wire separating us. "Linda, where have you been? I needed you."

"I'm sorry, Mom. Paul and I were at the lake. What's wrong?"

"Your brother—Jimmy's in the ICU."

My breath caught. "What happened?"

"He was coming home with his friends the night before last. He was asleep in the back of the van when the boys were hit head-on by a drunk driver."

I sat down hard in my kitchen chair. "Is he going to be all right?"

My mother tried to speak through her sobs. "The crash knocked a front wheel off the van, causing it to flip end over end. Jimmy was thrown out and landed on his chest. The impact crushed his lungs as well as his fifth and sixth thoracic vertebrae. He cracked his kidneys and tore his liver and spleen." She took a deep breath before she continued. "He's not expected to live through the night."

I gasped, and my mother spoke in a whisper, "The doctors said even if he does live, he'll be brain damaged. He'll never wake up or walk again."

I was absolutely stunned by this news—stunned such a thing could even happen and shocked it had happened to my nineteen-year-old brother.

That night, as I rushed to make plans to fly home to be with my family, I repeatedly cried out to God, *Dear Lord, help Jimmy!*

But as I shot up my desperate prayers, I wondered, *Does God hear me? Is a miracle even possible?*

—————

Perhaps you're where I was that long-ago night. A situation, need, or circumstance has caught you off guard and you long to call out to God for help, but you're wondering, *Does God even care about my trouble? Can I trust him in my time of difficulty? And if he can be trusted, why am I dealing with this crisis in the first place?*

Before I discuss the answers to your questions or tell you what happened to my brother, let's look at a conversation Jesus had with his disciples only hours before his death on the cross, a death only he knew was imminent. He was celebrating Passover with his friends when he spoke to them about the coming trouble, trouble the disciples did not expect and could not possibly comprehend.

After all, these men had seen the miracles Jesus had performed. They knew Jesus was the Son of God. They believed he would soon be crowned king of the Jews and elevated to both religious and political power, perhaps ruling Jerusalem as both high priest and king. Little did they understand that Jesus would soon wear a crown of *thorns*. They never dreamed that in a few hours Jesus's call to be king would lead him to hang on an old rugged cross until he was dead.

> *"Don't let your hearts be troubled. Trust in God, and trust also in me"*
>
> (John 14:1 NLT).

So what do you suppose he told these dear men who had left everything to follow him? He told them, "Don't let your hearts be troubled. Trust in God, and trust also in me" (John 14:1 NLT).

I wonder if Jesus's followers remembered those words when the Roman soldiers arrested Jesus and shortly thereafter executed him. I wonder if they contemplated those words as, in the aftermath of Christ's crucifixion, they hid in back rooms throughout the city, afraid for their very lives.

Probably not. But before we criticize the disciples for their shortsightedness, remember, they did not yet understand that Jesus had to die before he could be resurrected. They had no clue that Jesus's death would win our victory over both sin and death and seat Jesus next to the Father as the King of our hearts.

Welcoming the Presence of God

Are you facing a dark hour as you ponder your circumstances? If so, you have much in common with the disciples as they faced a crisis beyond their imaginations.

15

But take heart, the words Jesus shared with his friends as he prepared them to face trouble are the very words he longs to say to you. Take a deep breath and speak the words of Jesus aloud: "Don't let your hearts be troubled. Trust in God, and trust also in me."

Read these words again and nestle into them as you begin to rest in this command.

Next, reflect on this: *If you read this book until the end, you will experience miracles.*

I know that's a bold statement. But I really believe you'll experience miracles, not because you'll learn magical prayer formulas, though you will learn how to pray powerful prayers. I believe you will experience miracles because you will draw nearer to God and his presence. Miracles are not about praying the perfect prayer; miracles are about what happens when we welcome God's presence and power into our situations and our lives.

> *Miracles are not about praying the perfect prayer; miracles are about what happens when we welcome God's presence and power into our situations and our lives.*

So if you're facing a dilemma or a circumstance that needs a miracle, I have good news for you. If you allow him, God will use your pain as a key to open the door to himself. And it's in his presence that miracles happen.

Keep in mind, though the disciples experienced their darkest hour when they saw Jesus dead and buried, they soon experienced their most miraculous moment when they witnessed Jesus alive and risen from the dead a mere seventy-two or so hours later.

Only Jesus could flip his tragic death into a miracle that would free humankind from the dominion of Satan, sin, and death.

And because of Jesus's resurrection, the disciples could once again walk with him. But the bigger miracle is that, because of Jesus's resurrection, we too can walk with God.

Do you recall Jesus's parting words days after his resurrection and moments before he ascended into heaven? He told his disciples, "And surely I am with you always, to the very end of the age" (Matt. 28:20).

These words are also for you: And surely I am with you always.

Sarah Young, a missionary who actively listens for the Savior's voice as she studies Scripture, writes about these words of Jesus in her book *Jesus Calling*:

> I AM WITH YOU. These four words are like a safety net, protecting you from falling into despair. Because you are human, you will always have ups and downs in your life experience. But the promise of My Presence limits how far down you can go. Sometimes you may feel you are in a free fall, when people or things you have counted on let you down. Yet as soon as you remember that *I am with you,* your perspective changes radically. Instead of bemoaning your circumstances, you can look to Me for help. You recall that not only am I with you, *I am holding you by your right hand. I guide you with My counsel, and afterwards I will take you into Glory.*[1]

The presence of Jesus in our lives changes everything.

Knowing God

To abide in Christ, we must first know him.

Mona was furious when her daughter Trina called to tell her she was worried that if Mona were to die on the operating table during her upcoming knee surgery, she wouldn't go to heaven. Mona called her friend Joanie to complain. "Imagine!" Mona said. "I'm a good person. I've raised good children. How dare my own daughter think God would send me to hell."

Joanie told her, "Mona, did you know the key to going to heaven has nothing to do with being nice?"

"Of course it does. What are you talking about?"

"For starters, not everyone who goes to heaven *is* nice. Did you know many killers and thieves are in heaven?"

Mona was shocked. "Why would God put a murderer in heaven but not me?"

Joanie said, "Do you remember the thief on the cross next to Jesus?"

"Never heard of him."

Joanie pulled out her Bible and read from the book of Luke:

One of the criminals who hung there hurled insults at him: "Aren't you the Messiah? Save yourself and us!"

But the other criminal rebuked him. "Don't you fear God," he said, "since you are under the same sentence? We are punished justly, for we are getting what our deeds deserve. But this man has done nothing wrong."

Then he said, "Jesus, remember me when you come into your kingdom."

Jesus answered him, "Truly I tell you, today you will be with me in paradise." (23:39–43)

When Joanie finished reading the passage, Mona wailed, "That's not fair! Why would God forgive a thief? I love Jesus. Why wouldn't he accept me into heaven?"

Mona had a great question, one I'll answer with another great question: Could it be possible to "love" Jesus without "knowing" him?

Consider this. Let's say I'm a big fan of Oprah, and I just *love* her. Let's imagine I've watched her on TV for years, read every issue of her magazine, seen all of her movies, noted her philanthropic giving, and been impressed she started an entire TV network. But though I *love* all these things about her, we've never met. So are we friends?

Now let's say I've had a really bad day, so I decide to call Oprah so I can discuss my angst with her. I somehow find her private number and call her up and say, "Hi, Oprah. It's Linda, and I just *love* you. Got a minute?"

Imagine the silence that would hang on the line before she says, "Excuse me. Do I *know* you?"

"No, but that's okay because I just *love* you. Besides, I just wanted to chat."

Hello? What would compel Oprah to take time for my call when the two of us have no connection other than my knowledge of her fame?

> *Sadly, a person who has head knowledge about God's fame but has never taken the time to connect with him through prayer or pursue forgiveness of sins through Jesus does not have a relationship with him.*

In much the same way, I think it's possible to "love" God without ever bothering to connect with him. Sadly, a person who has head knowledge about God's fame but has never taken the time to connect with him through prayer or pursue forgiveness of sins through Jesus does not have a relationship with him.

So how can we connect with God?

The good news is that God, unlike most celebrities, *will* answer us when we call. And if we want a relationship with God, we *must* call upon him. Otherwise, he may tell you on the day you meet him on the other side of eternity, "I never knew you. Away from me" (Matt. 7:23).

That would be a tragedy, especially since Jesus has already given you the right and the privilege to connect with God through his great sacrifice for you.

So don't be offended that God accepts murderers and thieves into heaven; be glad. What this really means is that there is also room in his kingdom for the likes of you and me—for all of us. The good news is that the gospel is not about condemning the world (John 3:17); it's about Jesus rescuing whoever will believe in him (John 3:16).

You can begin a relationship with God with a simple prayer:

> *Dear Lord,*
>
> *Thank you that when I call upon you, you hear and answer me. Please forgive me of all my sins. Give me the power and the strength to turn from my sin as I turn to you. Thank you that Jesus died on the cross and rose from the dead so I can have forgiveness of sins and I can know you. Thank you that you now see me through the righteousness of Jesus. I give you my whole life. Help me to draw near to you as you draw near to me.*
>
> *In Jesus's name, amen.*

This is the first step in building an intimate relationship with God. But unless we receive the righteousness of Jesus, we will never be holy enough to walk (or be in relationship) with God. How amazing it is that we only have to ask, and Jesus will lend us his wonderful robe of righteousness to wear. When we slip into his righteousness, our sins are covered by the power of his blood. And the good news is that when God sees us dressed in the righteousness of his Son, he opens his arms to us so that we may walk with him. What a privilege and a blessing.

Rejoice that you know you have a relationship with God. But your job isn't done. Now it's time to grow in that relationship. The more you invite God into your life, the more you'll learn how to rest in his abiding presence and the more miracles you'll see.

One of the best ways to get to know God better is by talking to him. In fact, Andrew Murray, a South African teacher and pastor born in 1828, once said, "Abiding fully means praying much."[2]

But exactly what is prayer? Prayer is simply talking to God. It can include inviting or resting in his presence; thanking and worshiping him; asking for guidance and direction; asking for help, relief, and miracles; or just telling God about your day, worries, troubles, joys, fears, and frustrations.

But even beyond talking to God, your main goal should be to rest in his presence, for as O. Hallesby, a Lu-

> *Prayer is simply talking to God.*

theran professor from Norway, once said, "There come times when I have nothing more to tell God. If I were to continue to pray in words, I would have to repeat what I have already said. At such times it is wonderful to say to God, 'May I be in Thy presence, Lord? I have nothing more to say to Thee, but I do love to be in Thy presence.'"[3]

I'm so glad you picked up this book, and my prayer for you is that you'll learn how to be in God's presence as we discuss praying for miracles while we fight the good fight of faith.

At the end of each chapter, you will find a miraculous prayer for you to pray based on God's Word. Each prayer will lead you into a deeper intimacy with God, which is the place where miracles happen. Following that is a Scripture passage for you to read aloud and ponder. Faith comes by hearing, so use your own voice to read the Word so your faith will grow.

Miraculous Prayer

Dear Lord,
Thank you that you are a God who performs miracles and that
you display your power in mighty ways. Open my eyes so I can

not only see the miracles already surrounding me but also learn how to approach you for the miracles I'm desperate to receive.

I ask you to guide me, strengthen me, and show me you are near. In fact, Lord, I give you permission to enter every room in my life, including every secret place, longing, despair, need, and desire, with the holy light of your presence. Remind me always that you are with me, even when I feel alone. I've chosen to believe in you and to live my life resting in your presence, resting in the fact that my hope and trust are in you and you alone.

In Jesus's name, amen.

Scripture to Ponder

(Read aloud.)

> Blessed are those who have learned to acclaim you,
>   who walk in the light of your presence, LORD.
> They rejoice in your name all day long;
>   they celebrate your righteousness.

Psalm 89:15–16

To see Linda's interview about tips for praying for miracles, go to www.NeedMiracleBook.com or turn to page 206 for a QR code.

2

The Trust Factor

But I trust in you, LORD;
I say, "You are my God."

Psalm 31:14

Sometimes the only way we can learn how to trust God is to step into trouble. That's exactly what happened to me early one morning. I rolled out of bed, slipped into my robe and slippers, swung open the bedroom door, and stared, bleary eyed, into the hallway. I blinked. For some odd reason, the carpet looked shiny. *But why?* I blinked again and took a step, my foot sloshing in wetness. That's when it clicked. The hallway was covered in water.

I followed the river to the hallway bathroom, where a steady waterfall flowed from a clogged toilet. I jiggled the handle to turn off the flow then found my carpet-cleaning machine to suck up the water. As I pushed the cleaner's nozzle across the carpet, I couldn't help but notice the water was in endless supply. A little later, my husband opened the bedroom door and stepped into our soggy waterway. "What happened?" he asked.

"The toilet overflowed. I think it ran all night."

Paul asked, "What does it look like downstairs?"

My heart skipped a beat. *Downstairs?* I hadn't even thought to look there. Together we went to the basement. The scene looked straight out of a disaster movie. Part of the ceiling had caved in, ruining walls and cabinetry. That, combined with the catastrophe upstairs, meant over fourteen hundred square feet of our house lay in wet ruin.

> *How are we ever going to learn to walk on water if an occasional toilet doesn't overflow?*

Perhaps you've noticed it too; sometimes trouble comes in like a flood.

If you've ever been shocked by a circumstance of life, perhaps you've wondered, *If God loves me, why would he allow horrible things to happen in the first place?*

You may not realize it, but we actually live on a battlefield. That's why we not only trip over the wounded or dying but also at times get wounded ourselves by flying shrapnel. But when life gives us pain, we sometimes lift an eyebrow at God as if to say, *If you want me to trust you, why are you making it so difficult?*

But honestly, how are we ever going to learn to walk on water if an occasional toilet doesn't overflow? Could it be the Lord wants us to trust in him, regardless of the storms, shrapnel, or floods surging around us?

That's how the people in the Bible learned to trust God for miracles—by looking to him in times of trouble. Did you know trouble can be found in every book of the Bible? Even the beloved apostle Paul experienced difficulties. In fact, he once wrote his friends in the church in the city of Corinth:

We do not want you to be uninformed, brothers and sisters, about the troubles we experienced in the province of Asia. We were under great pressure, far beyond our ability to endure, so that we despaired of life itself. Indeed, we felt we had received the sentence of death. But this happened that we might not rely on ourselves but on God, who raises the dead. He has delivered us from such a deadly peril, and he will deliver us again. On him we have set our hope that he will continue to deliver us, as you help us by your prayers. Then many will give thanks on our behalf for the gracious favor granted us in answer to the prayers of many. (2 Cor. 1:8–11)

But if we're at war, why are so many people seemingly immune to the battle?

- It may not be their turn to fight the good fight.
- Not everyone is at war.

For those not at war, the reason may simply be this: the enemy (Lucifer himself) has these dear souls right where he wants them, in the perfect position to spend an eternity of torment with him.

Think of it this way. If the enemy lobbed the same kind of grenades at an unbeliever that he sometimes throws at you, the unbeliever might turn to God to seek comfort and help in his pain. So perhaps when God allows trouble into our lives, he is simply giving us the opportunity to seek him and to invite him to draw ever near.

So if you feel the need to call on God for help, count it as a good thing. David, in the days before he became king, often called out to God, especially when he was on the run from King Saul, a man who wanted him dead. It was on the battlefield that David learned to trust God with his whole heart. David wrote of his experiences in the Psalms: "With your help I can advance against a troop; with my God I can scale a wall" (18:29). David also said, "Surely God is my help; the Lord is the one who sustains me" (Ps. 54:4).

God is waiting in your trouble so he can teach you how to walk with him through the battlefield.

Is It Okay to Pray for Miracles?

I was flying home from St. Louis when I struck up a conversation with another believer. We had a lively discussion about whether it is okay to seek miracles, including relief from pain. Anna said, "What if pain is a gift God wants to give us so he can do a great work in us? But what if all we want to do is pray that gift away?"

This is a great question, a question I took to my friend and fellow author Rebekah Montgomery, who after being infected with West Nile virus some years ago has experienced great pain from partial paralysis in both her respiratory system and limbs. Rebekah confided, "The nights I experienced the greatest pain were the nights God pulled me closest to himself in the most exquisite ways."

I asked her, "Would you exchange those experiences with God for no pain?"

Rebekah hesitated. "That's a tough question. Though I would never want to give up those precious times I had with the Lord, I would certainly want to dial down the pain a few notches."

And indeed, as I had observed and even prayed with Rebekah during her most difficult bouts of pain, Rebekah was eager to gain relief not only from her pain but also from her paralysis and lack of breath. And who could blame her?

How I rejoiced with her when she found relief through treatments in a hyperbaric chamber. Those treatments were the miracle cure that put oxygen back into the parts of her body that were in painful atrophy. The treatments not only saved

Rebekah's life but also gave her back her breath and movement and lessened her pain.

Do I think God is displeased with Rebekah for her pursuit of health? Not at all. For as Rebekah has recovered, she's been able to minister to others and even to go on mission trips to Haiti. In other words, God turned both Rebekah's times of sickness and her times of health into miracles. Just as God used the pain in Rebekah's life to draw her near, he also used her healing to give her fresh purpose.

Rebekah asked me, "What about you? It couldn't have been easy on you when your baby was hurt in a car accident and spent a year in a coma. Would you be willing to go through all that again, especially if you thought it would draw both you and others closer to the Lord?"

> *Perhaps it's good that we don't get to pick our trials, because if we were honest, most of us would simply opt out.*

I felt a sheepish smile spread across my face. "I hate to disappoint you, Rebekah, but I'm more of a mother than a saint. Unlike what God did for us by giving up his only Son to torture and death, I don't think I could ever willingly *pick* giving up the well-being of my child."

"I understand," Rebekah said quietly.

"However," I continued, "I'm delighted God used my trial for his purposes. How I praise him that he was with me and taught me to trust him in my difficulties. So perhaps it's good that we don't get to pick our trials, because if we were honest, most of us would simply opt out."

But that said, I have to recognize there's a lot of evidence in God's Word to indicate that many of our trials are actually designed not by God but by our enemy, an enemy who comes to steal, kill, and destroy (John 10:10). In fact, Jesus even told

Simon Peter, "Simon, Simon, Satan has asked to sift all of you as wheat. But I have prayed for you, Simon, that your faith may not fail. And when you have turned back, strengthen your brothers" (Luke 22:31–32).

It was Satan who asked to sift Simon Peter and who even influenced him to deny Jesus. But because of Jesus's prayers, Simon Peter was able to repent and continue his journey with Christ and to strengthen not only his brothers but also us.

Then there's Job. In the book of Job, we learn that the terrible tragedies that befell this godly man were designed by Satan. Satan's goal was to see if Job would turn from God in the face of trouble. But through it all, Job stayed true to God and in the end even asked God to forgive him for his pride. In a true miracle, God blessed Job twice as much as before.

I believe the car accident that put my eighteen-month-old baby into a coma, before she awoke to a life of disabilities, was not designed by God but by the enemy. Though I do believe God allowed it to save the lives of the people who have viewed our story as an illustration of God's love. But as a mom, I would have been happy to have picked this result without picking the tragedy. But even so, how thankful I am that when Satan was given the opportunity to sift me, Jesus was at the right hand of the Father praying for me, just as he is also praying for you (Rom. 8:34).

I know many believers who, when they look back at times of tragedy in their lives, can see how God flipped their circumstances into a miracle—like the seventy-year-old woman I met from Akron, Ohio. Ruthie opened her wallet and pulled out a photo of her adult son with cerebral palsy. She told me, "I now know why God allowed my son to have CP. It was for me. My husband has now gone on to be with the Lord, but I still have my wonderful, loving son who lives with me. We go all over—on camping trips together." Ruthie beamed. "We have a wonderful life."

Another woman told me, "I too have a disabled child. People feel sorry for me when they see her. However, they have no idea of the love in my home, due in part because of my daughter's condition. If they knew, they would be jealous."

I can relate. What the enemy means for evil, God means for good, for the saving of many lives or even unexpected blessings. After all, God is in the miracle business, and often miracles come in disguise, like my disastrous house flood. After four months of living in a disruptive construction zone, I had new linoleum, carpet, paint, cabinetry, ceiling, and walls, plus a lovely update to my forty-year-old bathroom, all paid for by my insurance. Mind you, I wouldn't have picked this inconvenience, but nevertheless, it turned into a blessing, a blessing I would not have enjoyed except through the accidental overflow of a toilet.

Are Miracles Possible Today?

Are miracles possible today? The answer is yes, despite the fact that many people believe Jesus doesn't heal today. What we need to understand is that this way of thinking was first taught in seminaries during the last century. How else could professors explain why they themselves saw no miracles? However, despite this teaching, the miracles of Jesus have continued to appear throughout the world. In fact, I find today that a belief in miracles crosses denominational lines, mainly because miracles happen everywhere. I can personally testify and rejoice that God has done many miracles in my life. There have been emotional, spiritual, and physical miracles, including healing from migraines, neck and shoulder pain, and hypoglycemia. I've also witnessed miracles for others, many of which I'll share throughout the book.

But why does God perform miracles?

- to show his love for us
- to show his glory
- to show Jesus is Lord
- to bring people to faith
- for his good pleasure
- to fulfill a purpose
- to answer us when we call

However, God does not give us a magic wand so we can grant ourselves whatever we desire. If he did, we'd probably worship what we wanted God to do for us instead of worshiping God himself.

When Miracles Don't Happen

To help us learn how to pray for miracles, let's study why some miracles fail to appear. Philip Yancey, in his book *Prayer: Does It Make Any Difference?* tells a difficult story:

> A faith healer in the U.S. scheduled a crusade in Cambodia, a country with a tiny minority of Christians. Posters went up promising healing and miracles for any problem. Peasants sold their cows, even their houses and traveled to Phnon Penh for the rally. As a result of landmines left over from the Vietnam War, one in two hundred Cambodians is an amputee, and many of these flocked to the crusade as well. When the amputees were not healed, a riot broke out in the stadium. The evangelist had to be rescued by an army helicopter, which whisked him to the safety of a hotel. When the angry crowd poured out of the stadium and surrounded the hotel, the faith healer departed the country and returned to the U.S.

A church leader from Cambodia told Yancey, "You cannot imagine the impact on the struggling church in Cambodia. It has set us back at least fifty years. We may never recover credibility here."[1]

Many elements of this story disturb me. While I honestly don't think it was wrong to pray for the sick in Cambodia, God is not our puppet. We can't expect him to perform miracles simply to amuse a crowd or to make a name for ourselves. But that doesn't mean we shouldn't pray for others or humbly seek him regarding solutions to impossible situations. We should. There is an undeniable correlation between asking God for miracles and receiving them.

What about the question of whether God can heal an amputee? Though God has been known to restore limbs, most amputees will most likely remain so. Why?

In my book *When You Can't Find God: How to Ignite the Power of His Presence*, I share a story about the time my quadriplegic daughter heard that a friend had lost his faith because God didn't heal amputees. Realizing Laura was unfamiliar with the word *amputee*, but not wanting to be too graphic for my kindhearted daughter, I gently explained it meant dear ones who cannot use their arms or legs.

That's when Laura let me know that when she'd spent time in heaven after her accident, she'd seen people who couldn't use their arms and legs on earth who could use them in heaven.

Then it hit me. "Laura, were you one of those people?"

"Yes," she joyfully signaled to me.[2]

Laura's reaction shows that God's miracles can transcend our concepts of time and place, so an *unrealized* healing should be considered a *future* healing. That's why it upsets me when faith healers put the blame on the ill or injured whenever they are not instantly healed.

> *There is an undeniable correlation between asking God for miracles and receiving them.*

31

Thirty years ago I was visiting a Sunday school class taught by one of the pastors of a large church. During a question and answer session, an eighty-year-old woman slowly rose from her chair, leaning heavily on her cane. "What I want to know," she asked, "is why God hasn't healed my arthritic spine."

To my shock, the pastor looked at this dear woman with cold eyes and said, "The answer is simple. Obviously you don't have enough faith to be healed."

The old woman sat down crestfallen, and I was upset. If I hadn't been a visitor, I'm afraid I would have raised my hand and demanded that this pastor demonstrate his *own* faith by praying a prayer of healing for the old woman—right on the spot.

However, this story ends on a happy note. Because of the time that's transpired since this incident, this woman is no doubt now in eternity with Jesus, where, praise God, she no longer uses a cane or suffers from arthritis.

But let's revisit her question. It's true that many people find earthly healing, but not everyone. Why?

- Sometimes it *is* a matter of lack of faith. Did you know Jesus had trouble performing miracles in his hometown because the people there had such little faith? (See Mark 6:5.)
- So we can see God turn what the enemy meant for evil into good (see Gen. 50:20–21).
- So we can trust God when his will trumps our will (see Rom. 8:28).
- There is unfinished spiritual warfare (see Matt. 17:19–21).
- Sometimes soul blocks such as bitterness and unforgiveness prevent healing (see Heb. 12:15).
- Because of godlessness (see Heb. 12:16–17).

This is a great list; however, we'd better be careful not to use it to judge others in their suffering lest God decide to teach us whatever lesson he is teaching them. "Judge not, that you be not judged" (Matt. 7:1 RSV).

But the good news is that miracles *do* happen today. I've seen them, I've experienced them, and I love to pray for them, as can you. Speaking of miraculous prayer, at the end of this chapter I've included one of the greatest, most tried-and-true prayers for miracles one can pray. But don't turn ahead or you'll miss out on how to be prepared to pray it.

Proverbs 3:5–6 says, "Trust in the LORD with all your heart and lean not on your own understanding; in all your ways submit to him, and he will make your paths straight." Here are a few steps you can take that will help you trust God with all your heart, steps we will soon pray through.

1. Do a faith and sin check. If you have sin or bitterness in your heart, you may have a soul block. We will talk about how to deal with prayer blockage in another chapter.
2. Put your difficulty into proper perspective. What difficulty is bigger than God?
3. Give God your difficulty so it will be his problem and not yours.
4. Give God any remaining fear you have regarding your difficulty.
5. Accept that this situation now belongs to God and he is in it.
6. Relax. Know God has it covered.

I did not include spiritual warfare on this list. But no worries, a few chapters from now, we will learn how to practice this effective form of prayer as well.

Pray the following prayer to ready yourself to pray Scripture-based miracle prayers:

> *Dear Lord,*
>
> *Forgive me of my sins and help me to forgive others. Lord,*
> *I'd like you to meet my difficulty of _____.*
> *In you and your power, Lord, this difficulty has met its match.*
> *Therefore, I'm giving my difficulty to you. From here on out*
> *this is your problem, not mine. Therefore, I've nothing to fear*
> *because I also give my fear to you. I'm so glad my hope is in*
> *you, and I will not be disappointed. I'm so glad I put my trust*
> *in you and you have this difficulty covered. I give you my worry*
> *as I rest in you.*
>
> *In Jesus's name, amen.*

Miraculous Prayer

I love to pray Scripture as covenant prayer, and one of the most powerful covenant prayers we can pray is based on Psalm 91. Many have prayed this prayer daily over their lives and the lives of family members and have seen miraculous results. This prayer is also known as the soldier's prayer. One church in the town of Seadrift, Texas, used this psalm to pray for the fifty-two sons of their community who had left for the battlefields of World War II. Over twenty women met to pray this psalm daily, and God honored their prayers by sending all fifty-two men home unharmed.[3]

Below, I've paraphrased this psalm from the Message as a prayer for you to pray as often as you'd like. Note that whenever you see "my family" in this prayer, feel free to call out the individual names of your loved ones.

> *Dear God,*
>
> *You are my refuge. I trust in you and I'm safe! You rescue me*
> *and my family from hidden traps; you shield me from deadly*

hazards. Your huge outstretched arms protect me and my fam-ily—and under your arms I'm perfectly safe because your arms fend off all harm. My family and I fear nothing—

- *not wild wolves in the night*
- *not flying arrows in the day*
- *not disease prowling in the darkness*
- *not disaster erupting at high noon*

Even though others succumb all around, drop like flies right and left, no harm will even graze me or my family. I and my family will stand untouched, watch it all from a distance, and watch the wicked turn into corpses.

Yes, because of you, God, my refuge and my very own home, evil can't get close to me or my family; harm can't get through the door.

God has ordered his angels to guard me and my family wher-ever we go. If we stumble, the angels will catch us; their job is to keep us from falling. I and my family will walk unharmed among lions and snakes and kick young lions and serpents from the path.

God, you say, "If you'll hold on to me for dear life, I'll get you out of any trouble. I'll give you the best of care if you'll only get to know and trust me."

God, I say I believe you and am holding on to you for dear life. As I get to know you more, I thank you for getting me and my family out of trouble. Thank you that you are giving me and my family the best of care.

God, you say, "Call me and I'll answer. I'll be at your side in bad times; I'll rescue you, then throw you a party. I'll give you a long life and give you a long drink of salvation!"

God, I say I am calling on you. Thank you for answering me and being at my and my family's side. Thank you for rescuing me and my family. I celebrate you. Thank you for giving me and my family long life and salvation.

In Jesus's name, amen.

Scripture to Ponder

(Read aloud.)

> When I cry out to You,
>   then my enemies will turn back;
>   this I know, because God is for me.
> In God (I will praise His word),
>   in the LORD (I will praise His Word),
> in God I have put my trust;
>   I will not be afraid.
>   What can man do to me?
>
> Psalm 56:9–11 NJKV

To pray Psalm 91 with Linda and to watch Linda talk more about trusting God, go to www.NeedMiracleBook.com or turn to page 206 for a QR code.

3

The Love Factor

I have loved you, O my people, with an everlasting love; with loving-kindness I have drawn you to me.

Jeremiah 31:3 TLB

My hubby and I were visiting with another couple when Ron, the husband, mentioned he was in extreme pain because he'd strained his back shoveling snow. "I really did it this time," he said.

"Have you asked God to heal your back?" I asked.

Ron looked at me as if I had two heads. "I don't want to bother God with *that*," he confessed. "God's got a lot of other more important prayers to answer. He doesn't need me complaining about my back."

"When you begin to realize how much God wants to have a closer relationship with you, you might consider that he does want you to come to him with your pain," I told him.

Ron's wife, Meg, bobbed her head in agreement and said, "That's what I've been telling him."

I grinned. "Ron, would you permit us to pray for your back?" Ron shrugged. "Go ahead."

We bowed our heads, and I prayed a very simple prayer. "Lord, I know you care about Ron and his aching back. So, Lord, would you mind showing Ron he's not such a bother—by healing his pain?"

A day later Ron showed up at my door to see my husband. "How's your back?" I asked.

He shrugged. "Fine."

That's when the light dawned in his eyes. Because his back had stopped hurting, he'd forgotten about his pain as well as our prayer.

"Well, I'm really glad to hear it," I said as a sheepish grin spread across his face.

When you begin to realize how much God wants to have a closer relationship with you, you might consider that he does want you to come to him with your pain.

It was a great gotcha moment. But even better, God let Ron know it's okay to come to him with something as insignificant as an aching back.

Sometimes God answers our requests just to prove he cares. However, many people try to control God by praying prayers that essentially say, "God, if you don't answer my prayer the way I've instructed, then I'll be very unhappy with you. In fact, I may even stop believing in you."

That is the wrong attitude of prayer, for God cannot be blackmailed.

However, that was not the attitude in which I prayed for Ron. I believe God quickened my faith to boldly pray, just so he could make a point: God wants Ron—and all of us—to come to him. Period.

My friend Sue Cameron shares a story about a time God answered a simple prayer. In those days, Sue had three preschoolers and a tight budget. One afternoon, while shopping for groceries, she spotted a package of lovely soft, white, cotton socks. She really needed those socks, but when she looked at the price, she knew they weren't in her budget. With a sigh, Sue put the package of socks back into the display case and walked away. But as she did, she prayed a simple prayer. "God, I need socks."

The next day, Sue had an unexpected knock on her door, and when she opened it, she found her friend Shirley from church.

Shirley explained, "My daughter works for a sporting goods store, and sometimes they have overstocks, so I thought you could use these." Shirley thrust not one but three large garbage bags at Sue.

"Thanks for thinking of me," Sue said as Shirley hurried back to her car. When Sue opened that first bag, what do you suppose she found? It was filled with new, white, soft, lovely cotton socks.

Sue said, "I gathered my children into my arms—the children, not the socks—and hugged them. 'Isn't God good?'"[1]

Yes, he is.

So think of it. If God loves Ron enough to heal his aching back and Sue enough to give her three bags full of socks just because she happened to mention to him that she needed them, don't you think it's possible he might answer your prayers?

God Is Love

God loves you and wants a deeper relationship with you. God is a loving Father who is longing for us, his children, to be in a more meaningful relationship with him. Relationship is the reason he created us and why Jesus died and was resurrected; not because we're something special but because he *is* love (1 John 4:16) and because he first loved us (1 John 4:19).

How powerful is this love? Well, Romans 8:38–39 puts it this way: "For I am convinced that neither death nor life, neither angels nor demons, neither the present nor the future, nor any powers, neither height nor depth, nor anything else in all creation, will be able to separate us from the love of God that is in Christ Jesus our Lord."

The love the Father has for us was also demonstrated in the love Jesus had for his disciples. Consider what Jesus did for these twelve men the night before his crucifixion. An eyewitness, John the apostle, told it like this:

> Just before the Passover Feast, Jesus knew that the time had come to leave this world to go to the Father. Having loved his dear companions, he continued to love them right to the end. It was suppertime. The Devil by now had Judas, son of Simon the Iscariot, firmly in his grip, all set for the betrayal.
>
> Jesus knew that the Father had put him in complete charge of everything, that he came from God and was on his way back to God. So he got up from the supper table, set aside his robe, and put on an apron. Then he poured water into a basin and began to wash the feet of the disciples, drying them with his apron. When he got to Simon Peter, Peter said, "Master, you wash my feet?"
>
> Jesus answered, "You don't understand now what I'm doing, but it will be clear enough to you later." (John 13:1–7 Message)

God is a loving Father who is longing for us, his children, to be in a more meaningful relationship with him.

Imagine, Jesus, the only begotten Son of God, stooped to wash the stinky, smelly feet of the disciples as an act of love toward them. I don't know about you, but I don't often think of washing someone's feet. I mean, if your feet were really muddy, I might offer you my garden hose and maybe throw in a bar of soap. But sitting around worrying about someone else's stinky feet is not something I spend a lot of time thinking about.

However, foot washing was considered proper etiquette in those days. If a host had a dinner guest, he would send his servant in to wash the guest's feet before the meal. Maybe that's because people in those days dined by reclining on the floor. So when you think about it, a case of stinky feet could ruin everybody's meal.

But notice that instead of calling on a servant or even one of the disciples to wash everyone's feet, Jesus did it himself.

Just as Jesus loved the disciples enough to wash their feet, he loves us enough to wash us with his shed blood. That's the only way we can be holy enough to have a relationship with God, without the stench of sin spoiling our sweet fellowship.

"That's all well and good," you might say. "But I've had prayers that have gone unanswered; does that mean God doesn't love me?"

We've all experienced times when God did not answer our prayers the way we asked. But that doesn't mean God doesn't love us. It means that we need to allow God to be God. Consider what Nancy Bayless learned the last night of a two-year voyage.

Nancy and her husband, Lynn, had bought a thirty-foot sailboat in England, then followed Columbus's route across the Atlantic as they made their way back to their home in Fort Lauderdale. The last night of their trip, they decided to anchor on a pink and yellow coral reef that rested just beneath the surface of the calm waters of Gun Cay in the Bahamas. That evening, as Nancy and Lynn watched the sea turn sunset red, they felt blessed. But later, after they had crawled into their beds, thunder awakened them. A monstrous storm had churned the calm into waves that threatened to pound their boat into the razor-sharp coral bed to which they were anchored. As Nancy held the steering wheel, the boat's compass spun as one wave after another tried to sweep her husband over the deck. Nancy, realizing they might lose not only their boat but also their lives, felt as if God had turned his back on them. As the thunder boomed, Nancy screamed at God, "Stop this storm! Don't you know we're almost home? Why are you letting this happen?"

Only the wind replied, and Nancy's thoughts turned to the words Jesus spoke on the Mount of Olives: "Father, if you are willing, please take away this cup of horror from me. But I want your will, not mine" (Luke 22:42 TLB).

Guilt surged over her as she contemplated yet another Scripture passage: "No, I will not abandon you or leave you as orphans in the storm—I will come to you" (John 14:18 TLB).

That's when Nancy remembered all the times God had kept both her and her husband safe in the storms they'd encountered in their two-year journey. Nancy decided she wanted God's will, regardless of the cost. She humbly prayed, "Father, forgive me. Please let me feel your presence, please let me know your will."

Instantly, the storm lifted. Nancy and her husband were safe under a star-filled heaven. Later, as Nancy steered their boat into the dawn, she smiled, marveling at God's strength in her weakness, knowing she had witnessed God's unconditional love, which would weather her through all the storms of life.

I love the lesson Nancy learned as she prayed, recognizing and accepting God's will as well as his love for her.[2]

Reminders of God's Love

We all need to be reminded that God loves us and hasn't forgotten us. Isaiah 49:15–16 makes this clear: "[And the Lord answered] Can a woman forget her nursing child, that she should not have compassion on the son of her womb? Yes, they may forget, yet I will not forget you. Behold, I have indelibly imprinted (tattooed a picture of) you on the palm of each of My hands" (AMP).

After my brother's accident, my mother, in the moment she felt most abandoned by God, got a precious reminder that he was with her. Imagine her horror when she and my dad got that dreaded middle-of-the-night phone call while they were away visiting relatives. "Mrs. Evans," the doctor from the emergency room said to my mother, "I know you want to get home, but there's no need to speed. It's unlikely your son will be alive by the time you get here."

> *We all need to be reminded that God loves us and hasn't forgotten us.*

But my dad did speed through the darkness, making the four-hour trip in two and a half. Once at the hospital, my parents discovered that though Jimmy had survived surgery, he was in the direst of conditions.

Later that morning, while my parents huddled together in the ICU waiting room, the doctor came in and told them, "Your son's chances of survival are slim."

The doctor left, and my mother began to sob. That's when an old woman stood up from one of the waiting room chairs and walked across the room to her. The woman cooed, "Honey, now, don't you pay no attention to what they done told you. I've been talking to the Lord, and he tell me your boy going to be all right."

Later, my mom asked me, "Do you suppose the old woman was an angel?"

I do. Especially when you consider that the literal definition of "angel" is "a messenger sent from God." And that's exactly what my mother received in her darkest hour: God's message of hope. So whether the waiting room visitor was a prayerful believer or an angel sent from heaven, God saw that his message of hope was delivered.

That's so like God, always reminding us of his presence in any situation through a message, his Word, a good book, a sermon, or even a song of praise. If you ever find yourself in need of God's encouragement, know that your message of love is waiting for you as soon as you pick up your Bible, call your prayer circle, go to church, or sing as a sacrifice of praise unto the Lord.

No matter how dire your circumstances or how alone you feel, God will not abandon you.

Stormie Omartian, in her book *The Prayer That Changes Everything*, tells about the time in her life she felt unlovable. Though she craved love, she spurned it time and again. Stormie said, "I felt that when you love someone, you needed to offer them a whole person, and I knew that I wasn't."

But when she came to the Lord, Stormie could sense God's love, especially when she was with other believers. It became easy for her to believe God loved *them* but not *her*, because she still felt unworthy. But as she grew to know God, she began to understand the depth of his love, even for her. She observed, "He doesn't love us because we deserve it. He loves us because He is a God of love. That's who He *is*. He cannot be something He isn't. And He loves *you* because you are His creation and He is your heavenly Father. There is no way He cannot love *you*."[3]

So when you consider that our enemy's main goal is to rob us of our understanding of God's love, you get the idea that he's out to steal our very identity of who we are in Christ.

Our Identity in Christ

Not long ago, my friend Hope received a phony email asking her to log into her Yahoo account through a link embedded in the email. But when she clicked on the link, instead of taking her to the Yahoo website, the link secretly redirected her to a counterfeit website belonging to identity thieves. When Hope typed in her Yahoo password, the thieves had what they needed to steal her Yahoo email account, and since Hope used that same password for her Facebook account, they were able to steal that too. Imagine! They locked Hope out of her own Yahoo and Facebook accounts and sent emails to all of her friends, telling them she'd been robbed and was stranded in Spain. "Wire me $500 and I'll pay you back later."

> *The enemy wants us to believe that God's love, the very thing we were created for, doesn't belong to us.*

One of Hope's friends did send the wire, never to see her money again.

So think of it, in the power of Hope's name and password, these thieves robbed Hope of her online identity and robbed her friend of her money.

The enemy is an identity thief. He wants us to believe that God's love, the very thing we were created for, doesn't belong to us. But believing this lie is paramount to giving the enemy the password that will rob us of our identity in Christ. For if we believe God loves everyone but us, we quit believing God will answer our prayers, and we may even stop praying all together. We'll mistakenly resign ourselves to the "fact" that either God is angry with us or he just doesn't care.

Don't allow the enemy to rip you off. The only way to make sure the enemy never steals your identity is to be sure you understand who you are in Christ. Here are a few clues.

1. You are loved: "For God so loved the world that he gave his one and only Son, that whoever believes in him shall not perish but have eternal life" (John 3:16).

45

2. You are forgiven: "I am writing to you, dear children, because your sins have been forgiven on account of his name" (1 John 2:12).
3. You are righteous: "God made him who had no sin to be sin for us, so that in him we might become the righteousness of God" (2 Cor. 5:21).
4. You are justified: "All are justified freely by his grace through the redemption that came by Christ Jesus" (Rom. 3:24).
5. You are in Christ: "God raised us up with Christ and seated us with him in the heavenly realms in Christ Jesus" (Eph. 2:6).
6. Christ is in you: "To them God has chosen to make known among the Gentiles the glorious riches of this mystery, which is Christ in you, the hope of glory" (Col. 1:27).
7. You are not condemned: "Therefore, there is now no condemnation for those who are in Christ Jesus" (Rom. 8:1).
8. You are an overcomer: "You, dear children, are from God and have overcome them, because the one who is in you is greater than the one who is in the world" (1 John 4:4).
9. You are more than a conqueror: "In all these things we are more than conquerors through him who loved us" (Rom. 8:37).
10. You are a victor: "For everyone born of God overcomes the world. This is the victory that has overcome the world, even our faith" (1 John 5:4).

Do you know that you, personally, do not have to *be* these things on your own? In Christ, you *are* these things. But if you are still struggling with any of these concepts, then you need to renew your mind with the Word. Select the principles you are struggling with and reread their corresponding Scripture passages aloud. Reread and meditate on each passage you need to believe—until Scripture ignites your spirit. As you meditate on the Word in this way, it will renew your mind and you'll begin to believe in who you are in Christ Jesus, namely, *loved*.

Yes, dear friend, you are loved. Zephaniah 3:17 says, "The LORD your God is living among you. He is a mighty savior. He will take delight in you with gladness. With his love, he will calm all your fears. He will rejoice over you with joyful songs" (NLT).

The love factor is simply this: God loves you, and therefore, you have the right (through and in Jesus) to approach the throne of grace and to give God your requests.

We will talk more about how to give God your requests, but know that you have not only his permission to do so but also his blessing.

For as Paul said in Hebrews, "Let us then approach God's throne of grace with confidence, so that we may receive mercy and find grace to help us in our time of need" (4:16).

Miraculous Prayer

Dear Lord,

Thank you that you rejoice over us with singing.

Through Christ, we're more than conquerors. For neither death nor life, neither angels nor demons, neither the present nor the future, nor any powers, neither height nor depth, nor anything else in all creation, will be able to separate us from the love of God that is in Christ Jesus our Lord.

Thank you that this principle of love applies even to me. Thank you that I can approach your throne of grace with confidence so I may receive mercy and find grace in my time of need. Therefore, I bring you my need of _____ and ask you to provide a miracle.

In Jesus's name, amen.

Scripture to Ponder

(Read aloud.)

No, I will not abandon you or leave you as orphans in the storm—I will come to you.

John 14:18 TLB

To watch Linda interview Lisa Harper, go to www.Need MiracleBook.com or turn to page 206 for a QR code.

4

The Truth Factor

If you abide in My word, you are My disciples indeed. And you shall know the truth, and the truth shall make you free.

John 8:31–32 NKJV

What Is Truth?

Recently, my son took a university philosophy class in which he was assigned to write a term paper on the topic "Is man a machine?" questioning a sixteenth-century idea from the father of modern philosophy, René Descartes. When Jim approached his professor to clarify his assignment, the professor warned him not to write about "the soul" or "life," because everyone knows these two concepts are no longer considered true.

Excuse me? How sad an existence one has who not only takes God out of the equation but also removes the *who* of who we are (our soul) and then denies we even exist.

When I questioned Jim about his professor's ideas, Jim explained that he daily peppers his lectures with misquoted Scripture, giving his talks the ring of truth but without the presence of truth, a deadly and deceptive combo.

So I was interested in how my son would approach his term paper. He did so by theorizing that not only is man not a machine but also a machine is not a man. He explained there's really no such thing as AI (artificial intelligence), because a computer program does not have the awareness or self-intelligence to create itself and therefore must have a creator. As an example, Jim pointed out that the Watson, the IBM computer touted as the perfect example of modern AI technology, is noted for its ability to quickly answer Jeopardy-level questions. It's designed to rival the human mind's ability to understand the actual meaning behind words, distinguish between relevant and irrelevant content, and ultimately, demonstrate confidence to deliver precise final answers.

> *The truth is that the almighty God designed and created us for a divine purpose: to love and to be loved.*

Jim said, "IBM would argue that their program is exactly like a human competitor. However, my opinion is that their machine takes all the data, and brute force calculates the most likely answer. In other words, their machine has a really good dictionary and just looks to see what matches the most. No real intelligence is behind the Watson. Everything the machine does is derived from an equation designed by a programmer."

So if a machine or a computer program must be designed by an intelligent creator, then do you think it's possible we humans have also been designed by an intelligent Creator?

The truth is that the almighty God designed and created us for a divine purpose: to love and to be loved. We're not mistakes.

We're alive and we have a soul, a soul we can open to God's very presence.

The Bible refers to God as "the God of truth" (Ps. 31:5), the Holy Spirit as the "Spirit of truth" (John 15:26), and Jesus as "the truth" (John 14:6).

How to Live in Truth

My dear friend and author Debbie Alsdorf, in her book *A Different Kind of Wild*, shares her mother's last words to her. After glimpsing heaven, Debbie's mom told her, "Live like it's real—because it is."[1]

I love this truth. It's critical that we live our lives as though everything we know about God is real.

One way to live in truth is to read Scripture to renew our minds. In fact, Paul said in 2 Timothy 3:16–17, "All Scripture is given by inspiration of God, and is profitable for doctrine, for reproof, for correction, for instruction in righteousness, that the man of God may be complete, thoroughly equipped for every good work" (NKJV).

I'm going to repeat the importance of reading God's Word throughout this book, because daily reading of God's Word may be the most effective way to hear God speak specifically into our lives and circumstances. For example, imagine you have to face your irate boss over a matter that's beyond your control. You've stewed about how you'll respond to his angry prodding, and you're not sure you can make it through the meeting without a meltdown. Over lunch, you pull out your Bible, and a Scripture passage jumps off the page at you: "I can do all this through him who gives me strength" (Phil. 4:13).

The words quicken your spirit, and you realize you will make it through this meeting, not in your own strength but in God's. You suddenly find yourself at peace, ready to meet with your boss. An hour later, your supernatural peace overflows into the room, soothing not only you but also the tone of the meeting and leaving both your cool and your job intact.

God's Word can come alive and quicken your spirit even when the passage doesn't speak specifically to your situation. For example, in the previous illustration, the Scripture passage did not say, "Hey, you! Just because you have to meet with your difficult boss today, don't fear. God will give you the power to see you through the meeting."

But that doesn't matter. When Scripture comes alive, it illuminates truth in a way you can apply directly to the situation you are facing. However, if you don't pick up your Bible, you will not have the opportunity to connect to this power. If you need a miracle, how can you risk losing out on that kind of divine revelation?

> *When Scripture comes alive, it illuminates truth in a way you can apply directly to the situation you are facing.*

In addition to renewing our minds with Scripture, it's important to put on the belt of truth. Ephesians 6:14 says, "Stand firm then, with the belt of truth buckled around your waist."

I now daily pray for the armor of God in my life: the helmet of salvation, the breastplate of righteousness, the belt of truth, the shoes of the gospel of peace, the shield of faith, as well as the sword of the spirit (Eph. 6:13–17).

I understand the urgency to buckle God's truth around me as never before. If you've read my book *When You Can't Find God*, you may remember a great difficulty that befell me just as I finished my manuscript. Suddenly, the words I'd written turned into a letter from God to me, helping me through a startling trouble. You see, I'd made the shocking discovery that a woman I'd considered a close friend was in fact a professional con artist.

I thank God for shedding his light into this situation when he did. I believe the light turned on because as I began daily to put on the belt of truth, God opened my eyes and illuminated the lie that surrounded me. That's how I was able to stop the deception against me as well as against several other Christian authors before additional harm was done.

Sure, I took a financial hit when print runs, web pages, and media campaigns were never realized, and I also took an emotional hit with the discovery that a person I had considered a trusted friend was not only stealing from me, but had even gone so far as to embed spyware into my laptop in order to read my emails and to eavesdrop on my private conversations with my prayer partners so she could pretend to be the answer to my prayers.

But despite these painful hits, I never lost my identity in Christ. God and his truth as well as his comfort saw me through. So the real victim in this story is the con artist, a woman entangled in both self- and spiritual deception. Her loss, though not financial, is actually much greater than mine. I continue to pray God's truth will set her free.

Another reason to live in truth is that it protects us from deadly spiritual deception. I once heard an account of a man who had a counterfeit faith that consisted of a knowledge of God without knowing God. When he suddenly died, he found himself surrounded by demons who dragged him into hell. The demons laughed and said, "We deceived you and kept you from knowing the truth about God. Now you belong to us forever."

Thankfully, this man was resuscitated and tells his story as a warning to others. But this illustration shows the importance of understanding God's truth. And the good news is that God is willing to show us his truth if we but ask. David said in Psalm 25:4–5, "Show me your ways, LORD, teach me your paths. Guide me in your truth and teach me, for you are God my Savior, and my hope is in you all day long."

Asking for God's truth and guidance in our lives is the number one way we can defeat the enemy's attempts to deceive us.

I continue to seek God's truth in my life every day. In fact, I recently asked God to open my eyes to show me if there were any barriers preventing me from going deeper into my relationship with him.

> *Asking for God's truth and guidance in our lives is the number one way we can defeat the enemy's attempts to deceive us.*

As I was quietly listening for his still, small voice, he said, "It's good you have given me your bitterness and worries and have tapped into my strength to forgive others. But why haven't you given me your emotional pain?"

I instantly knew what he meant. In the years since my daughter's accident and resulting disability, I'd come to think of my continued pain as a cross I needed to carry myself. But as I became aware of the truth God was showing me, I saw in my mind's eye a whip lashing Jesus's back, with each strike resulting in a great wound.

God spoke to me gently. "As the Word says, 'By my stripes you are healed.' I've already taken your emotional pain in the wounding of my Son."

I was stunned as I realized that God, through Jesus, had also paid for my emotional wounds through the wounds of Jesus. I gasped as God spoke to me again. "Do you believe I *will* take your pain?"

I responded, "I believe you *could*."

He asked me, "But do you believe I *will*?"

Tears seeped from the corners of my eyes as I answered, "Yes. I choose to believe you *will*."

"Then I will replace your pain with more of my presence in your life."

In that moment, God began to show me pictures, like a slide show, of all the pain I'd been carrying. With each revelation, I prayerfully traded my painful wound for more of God's presence and joy. So can you. Pray:

> *Dear Lord,*
>
> *Just as you did for Linda, I ask you to trade my woundedness for more of your presence and joy. I know it is your will that I make this trade. So in your power and strength, help me to let go of my pain and give it to you. For by his stripes I'm healed.*
>
> *In Jesus's name, amen.*

God's Will

Speaking of God's will, how do we know it?

Now that's a great question, a question Jesus addressed when he taught us to pray in the Lord's Prayer. He kicked off his lesson by saying, "Pray along these lines: 'Our Father in heaven, we honor your holy name. We ask that your kingdom will come now. May your will be done here on earth, just as it is in heaven'" (Matt. 6:9–10 TLB).

Not only did Jesus teach us to ask for God's will, but he himself also asked for God's will when he prayed on the Mount of Olives the evening before his crucifixion. We read in Luke, "He knelt down and began to pray, saying, 'Father, if You are willing, remove this cup from Me; yet not My will, but Yours be done'" (22:41–42 NASB).

In this case, it *was* God's will to see Jesus drink from the cup of death set before him. And remarkably, Jesus willingly did so to save many people, including us.

I think "the saving of many people" is a clue to understanding God's will. Take a look at the life of Joseph, the young man who wore a coat of many colors to indicate he was his father's favorite. However, being his father's favorite did nothing to save him from a life filled with what must have seemed like one unanswered prayer after another. Joseph was sold into slavery by his brothers, falsely accused of a crime he didn't commit, and finally thrown into jail. But through it all, Joseph trusted God.

Not only did Jesus teach us to ask for God's will, but he himself also asked for God's will when he prayed on the Mount of Olives the evening before his crucifixion.

But the moment came when God finally answered his prayers and Joseph rose to power as second in command to the pharaoh of Egypt, to oversee and store provisions for the coming famine.

So when Joseph's own brothers came to him begging for grain, Joseph could have taken revenge. After all, weren't Joseph's brothers the root cause of his suffering and heartache? Perhaps, but Joseph recognized that God had granted his rise to power not in spite of the betrayal of his brothers but because of it. He even said so. "As far as I am concerned, God turned into good what you meant for evil, for he brought me to this high position I have today so that I could save the lives of many people" (Gen. 50:20 TLB).

Could it be that God says no to our prayers when his divine purpose for our trouble is to accomplish things such as saving the lives of many people?

Perhaps we need to pray as Jesus did, prayerfully seeking God's will over our own, then trusting that God's answer will bring us even greater miracles to better accomplish his purposes, like the saving of many lives.

This discussion takes me back to that horrific car crash when I hovered over my daughter's body. Kneeling in the mud, I called out to God in prayer. "Please, don't let Laura die. Please, don't let Laura be brain damaged."

I continued to call out these prayers night and day, for days, then weeks, then months. I felt certain God would answer. How I rejoiced when a year later, at the exact moment we put Laura's baby brother into her arms, Laura finally awoke from her coma.

Yet many of my prayers remained unanswered. Laura was still paralyzed, brain damaged, and on life support. How could this new norm be God's will?

I didn't believe it was, so I pleaded, I begged, and I tried to convince God I had enough faith for Laura's total healing. But God seemed to turn a deaf ear to my endless prayers and countless confessions of faith for Laura to be whole.

But when I look back, I see God's hand, a hand I would have too easily shrugged away. Today I believe God used my daughter's difficult journey to bring a family member back to faith.

Mere months before the accident, this beloved member of my family confided to me that she'd lost her faith. She challenged, "I bet you would turn your back on God if something should happen to your husband."

"It would be hard," I said. "But I would still follow God if something happened to Paul."

Alice frowned and stared into my eyes. "I believe you would. But what if something happened to your baby? I bet you would turn away then."

My breath caught. "That would be unimaginable. But if something happened to Laura, I would still follow God."

Little did I know I would soon have to live my words.

But I'm assured Alice, who watched me as I followed God through this tragedy, is in heaven today, in part because she read my life as though it were a Bible. I'm glad God used what happened to reach Alice. I now see it was the only way he could save her life.

So now the question is this: Would you walk through a difficulty if you knew God was using it to save your life, someone else's life, or even many lives?

Though it might be hard to say yes, the eternal results would certainly be worth it.

Is God's Will Always No?

I have good news. It is not always God's will to say no. We see that when the leper fell at Jesus's feet and asked, "If You are willing, You can make me clean" (Mark 1:40 NKJV).

How did Jesus respond?

"Then Jesus, moved with compassion, stretched out His hand and touched him, and said to him, 'I am willing; be cleansed'" (v. 41 NKJV).

But how do we know when our prayer requests are in fact God's will?

Sometimes we don't know, and that's where trust comes in. Evangelist Dwight L. Moody put it this way: "Spread out your petition before God, and then say, 'Thy will, not mine, be done.' The sweetest lesson I have ever learned in God's school is to let the Lord choose for me."[2]

That takes a deeper level of trust, and perhaps that's the point.

Sometimes God is silent concerning his will, and other times he quickens our spirit so we know his answer is yes! Romans 12:2 says, "Do not conform to the pattern of this world, but be transformed by the renewing of your mind. Then you will be able to test and approve what God's will is—his good, pleasing and perfect will."

When you've renewed your mind, then tested God's will, it's easy to believe God will move. Consider the woman who touched the hem of Jesus's garment.

And a woman who had been suffering from a hemorrhage for twelve years, came up behind Him and touched the fringe of His cloak; for she was saying to herself, "If I only touch His garment, I shall get well." But Jesus turning and seeing her said, "Daughter, take courage; your faith has made you well." At once the woman was made well. (Matt. 9:20–22 NASB)

You've got to love this story of the dear woman who was too timid to ask Jesus to heal her, yet because she'd seen Jesus heal others, she knew if she could just quietly reach out to him, she would get the miracle she so desperately needed.

How did she know that? In this case, she saw what Jesus could do, and her faith was quickened.

This recently happened to me. The same afternoon God told me he was willing to heal my emotional pain, my friend Carole called to tell me she'd been skiing down Aspen Mountain and on her first run of the day an out-of-control skier plowed into her from behind.

"She hit me so hard my skis flew off and landed with my poles down the mountain."

Carole was both dazed and surprised she had no broken bones. She told me, "I've been in car accidents that didn't hurt like this. My ribs are excruciatingly sore, and the pain is radiating to my chest. I can't bend my thumb, which means I won't be able to use my computer for weeks. Tomorrow I am going to be black and blue."

It was in that moment God quickened my spirit and showed me he wanted to heal Carole. I wish I knew how I knew. Perhaps it was because I had just seen him heal my emotional wounds and my faith level was soaring. Or perhaps the Holy Spirit himself quickened my spirit. Regardless, I was certain God was about to move on Carole's behalf, so I asked, "Do you think God has ever healed anyone from the kind of injuries you received on the slope today?"

"I don't know. Probably. What do you think?"

"I think he has. Do you think if God healed you it would *prevent* him from saving others?"

"I don't see how."

"Then, do you think God *will* heal you?"

"I think he *could*."

"But do you think he *will*?"

"I don't know."

I said, "What if it is God's will to heal you, but your level of faith will determine whether he does or not. What would you say then?"

Her faith quickened, and she said, "I would say God *will* heal me."

We prayed, "God, we believe it is your will to heal Carole. We believe her pain is lifting now, and tomorrow when she wakes up, she will not have a single bruise."

Instantly, after the prayer, Carole's thumb stopped throbbing, and the redness and swelling began to disappear. She said, "I feel the pain lifting."

The next morning, she reported that she did not have a single bruise. She said, "Do you know what a miracle that is?"

Our understanding of God's will is often a mystery, but a mystery we should continue to press to discover.

What a joy that God healed Carole from her injuries. But can I turn what happened to Carole into a surefire formula? I don't think so. Our understanding of God's will is often a mystery, but a mystery we should continue to press to discover.

Recently, my husband and I were in a prayer circle, and when it was my turn to pray, I felt led to pray for a gentleman in our group who'd been struggling with intense back pain for weeks. He hadn't asked me to pray, but I charged ahead anyway. As he seemed uncomfortable, I made my prayer quick. "Dear Lord, we know you are able, so we come to you to ask, please heal Sam's back, in the power and authority of the name and blood of Jesus."

Sam left the meeting without mentioning my prayer, so I was surprised when a couple of weeks later, when my husband and I ran into him at the market, he confided, "Linda, I have to tell you that I felt uneasy when you were praying for my back, but then I decided to quietly pray with you. I silently told the Lord, 'I don't have enough faith to pray for my back, but could you meet me where I am?'"

Sam grinned. "Here's the news. It was in that moment that God healed my back. I haven't had any pain since."

I love how Sam pressed into discovering God's will by asking God to meet him where he was, and as it turns out, God did. That leads me to ask, what if God is waiting to meet you where you are? Let's find out as we pray:

> *Dear Lord,*
> *I ask to be in your will as I come to you with my prayer request for _____. However, I'm not certain that I have enough faith to believe. Could you please quicken my faith and meet me where I am? Thank you!*
> *I pray this in both your will and in the power and authority of the name and blood of Jesus.*
> *Amen.*

What an exciting prayer. Take a minute to rejoice in the Lord.

Can We Lose a Miracle?

We can lose a miracle if we refuse to believe. For example, after the Israelites had crossed the desert, God had Moses send twelve spies into the Promised Land in order to bring his people a report on both the land and its inhabitants. But though the spies praised the fruit of the land, they complained that the land's inhabitants were fierce giants. Hearing this report, the people were afraid, and they cried, "Giants? Then we *can't* possess the land!"

But Caleb, one of the spies, argued, "We should go up and take possession of the land, for we can certainly do it" (Num. 13:30).

The people failed to understand that the Lord had *already* given them the land, not in their strength but in his. All they had to do was follow him into the land, and he would do the rest.

> *Keep pressing into him, keep seeking the truth of his will, then learn to trust him as you believe he is able and will do what he says he will do.*

It's interesting to note that the people got exactly what they *said*. The people who said, "We can't possess the land," didn't. Only the ones who saw the truth of the situation and said they *could* possess the land did.

So let's get this straight. The truth of how God wants us to pray for the miraculous follows these principles:

1. God wants us to pray in truth (John 14:15–17)—Know whom you are praying to (God) and through (Jesus).
2. God wants us to pray in his will (Matt. 6:9–10)—Ask God to show you his will in the matter.
3. God wants us to pray in trust (Ps. 31:14)—Trust him with his answer, no matter what.
4. God wants us to pray in faith (Matt. 17:20)—Pray believing he is able and will do what he says he will do.

Keep pressing into him, keep seeking the truth of his will, then learn to trust him as you believe he is able and will do what he says he will do.

ℳiraculous Prayer

Dear Lord,

I come to you in truth. I know who you are, the great God and Creator who designed and loves me. I come to you through the shed blood of Jesus.

Please show me your will and renew my mind to know your will. Quicken my spirit to see your will as I pray about

_____.

I ask you to turn _____ into a miracle. I trust you with the result.

I praise you, for I know you're able to do even more than I request. Therefore, I believe. Help my unbelief and meet me where I am. I believe you will do what you say you will do.

In Jesus's name, amen.

𝒮cripture to Ponder

(Read aloud.)

> The Lord is righteous in all his ways
> and faithful in all he does.
> The Lord is near to all who call on him,
> to all who call on him in truth.
> He fulfills the desires of those who fear him;
> he hears their cry and saves them.
> The Lord watches over all who love him,
> but all the wicked he will destroy.
>
> Psalm 145:17–20

Watch Linda's interview at www.NeedMiracleBook.com or turn to page 206 for a QR code.

5

The Forgiveness Factor

And be kind to one another, tenderhearted, forgiving one another, even as God in Christ forgave you.

Ephesians 4:32 NKJV

Most people would never add a few drops of arsenic to their fruit smoothie. They'd say, "That's just crazy."

Yet many sip daily from a cup of bitterness. And if you asked about it, they'd say, "Why shouldn't I? Didn't you see what my [friend, spouse, in-law, boss, employee, office, church, school, community, sweetheart, government, enemy, attacker, customer, neighbor, family member, or other] did to me? I never deserved *that*. So of course I sip from a bitter cup."

Sigh. We've all been there. However, it's been said that bitterness is the only poison one can drink with the mistaken assumption that the act of drinking it will harm someone else. And the truth is that we die a little every time we let bitterness seep into our thought life.

So I have to ask, if holding a well-deserved grudge is so harmless, then why did Jesus make statements such as, "And when you stand praying, if you hold anything against anyone, forgive them, so that your Father in heaven may forgive you your sins" (Mark 11:25).

Hey, I'm no legalist, but these words of Jesus are difficult to absorb because they seem to imply that Jesus, who we know forgives us freely (Rom. 3:24), could withhold his forgiveness if we choose to withhold ours.

This shows that Jesus is, at the very least, very earnest for us to forgive others. To take a closer look, let's consider Jesus's parable in which he compared the kingdom of heaven to a king who, while balancing his checkbook, discovered that one of his debtors owed him ten million dollars. When the debtor couldn't pay, the king ordered that he and his family and all he owned be sold to pay the debt. But the man fell on his face and begged, "Be patient with me and I will pay it all."

> *Bitterness is the only poison one can drink with the mistaken assumption that the act of drinking it will harm someone else.*

The king was filled with pity for him, released him, and forgave his debt simply because he asked. But the man soon accosted another fellow who owed him $2,000. He grabbed this fellow by the throat and demanded immediate payment. But the fellow fell down before the man and begged for more time. "Be patient and I will pay it."

But instead of having pity, the forgiven man had his debtor arrested and jailed until he could pay his bill in full.

When the king heard about what had happened, he called in the man he'd forgiven and said, "You evil-hearted wretch! Here I forgave you all that tremendous debt, just because you asked me to—shouldn't you have mercy on others, just as I had mercy on you?" (Matt. 18:32–33 TLB).

The angry king sent the man to the torture chamber until he paid every last penny due.

Jesus said, at the end of the story, "So shall my heavenly Father do to you if you refuse to truly forgive your brothers" (Matt. 18:35 TLB).

Who can blame Jesus for being serious that we forgive others? Look what he went through to forgive us. According to this parable, he forgives us just because we ask. But the kicker is, he wants us to forgive others. *But how?*

First, let's take a look at what it means to forgive. According to Dictionary.com, the meaning of *forgive* is:

1. to cease to blame or hold resentment against (someone or something)
2. to grant pardon for (a mistake, wrongdoing, etc.)
3. to free or pardon (someone) from penalty

That sounds like a tall order, one that, in some cases, would be impossible, right? Let's do a case study before we decide. Consider the true story of Darla.

Darla is a lovely young woman from Malaysia. She came to the United States when she was eighteen years old to fulfill her dream of attending a Christian college. That's how she found herself at a small Florida college, a darling girl every young man on campus noticed. And despite their attention, she was very careful to protect the one thing that was most important to her: her purity. She cherished her innocence, her love for the Lord, and the dear young man who'd recently asked her to be his wife.

One day, Ted, her fiancé, asked his best friend, Cody, if he'd escort Darla from the baseball game back to her dorm while he interviewed the players for the school paper.

Little did Ted or Darla know that Cody was in fact a violent sexual predator. On the way home Cody attacked Darla. In his car, Cody took Darla's purity, though she begged him to let her go. The assault was brutal, violent, and demeaning, and it broke Darla's heart. It also prompted her first of many suicide attempts that very evening.

Now, over a decade later, Darla stood before me, shaking as though the attack had occurred only the week before. As she tried to tell me what had happened, she fell into my arms, sobbing. "How could Cody do that to me? He took away my purity and innocence. Now I am nothing but *trash*."

A story like this makes our blood boil. There's no way we could ever justify what Cody did to Darla. His actions were wrong. Period. In fact, the assault had long-term effects, damaging every area of Darla's life: her marriage, faith, self-esteem, and even her will to live.

Darla's story begs the question: Aren't there limits to what God expects of us? Why would he want us to forgive someone who committed this level of wrong? And in truth, you may be wondering if God really requires Darla to forgive Cody at all.

Though I'm tempted to agree, I think God had some good reasons for leading Darla to the miracle of freedom from her bitterness, reasons we'll soon discuss. Following that, we'll discover how to forgive, even when it seems impossible to do so.

But let's start with the benefits of forgiveness. What do we gain when we forgive others?

Benefits of Forgiveness

Besides the fact that Jesus commands us to forgive others, the benefits include:

- more answered prayers
- being right with God both now and in eternity
- better emotional and physical health
- it changes eternity

More Answered Prayers

Dwight L. Moody once said, "I firmly believe a great many prayers are not answered because we're not willing to forgive someone."[1]

That's quite a statement, but Moody might be right. For example, I found that after the con artist stole money from me, I was able to forgive her, not through my power, but through God's power. Then, when I appealed to God to help me through the financial loss, he miraculously blessed me, providing new finances that doubly replaced what I'd lost. But I'm not so sure if God would have blessed me if I hadn't let go of my right to be bitter and forgiven the one who had committed this crime against me.

For many of us, bitterness *is* a barrier that keeps us from drawing nearer to God and receiving the

> *"I firmly believe a great many prayers are not answered because we're not willing to forgive someone."*

miracles we long for. Imagine it like this. Suppose you've been grievously wronged, and the person who wronged you begins to creep into your thoughts. But you justify your obsession because you're still busy mopping up the trouble he caused you. However, if you're not careful, here's what can happen. The bitterness you carry will begin to smell (spiritually and emotionally speaking) as though you were lugging a dead person around with you.

Imagine that one day you look up to see Jesus with his arms outstretched toward you. You smile, so wanting to draw near to him, so wanting his comfort in exchange for your pain. But you discover you can't reach back. Your arms are full of bitterness and death. You withdraw, wishing Jesus would do something to help. But as you turn away, you see a great sadness in his eyes, a look you count as rejection. Now, because it seems Jesus wasn't available to help you in your pain, you begin to believe your bitterness is the cross you must bear yourself.

But Jesus hasn't turned away from you; you've turned away from him. Your own bitterness has become the barrier between you and the Lord. And try as you might, you discover it's hard to draw near to his presence, offer your prayers, or even trust him when you can't find relief from your bitter thoughts. But what you may not realize is this: Jesus has not left you. He's still standing with his arms outstretched, hoping you'll put your bitterness where it belongs—in his arms. His dying on the cross for you has earned him the right, don't you think?

If you'd give him your bitterness, you'd be free to draw nearer to him and to feel his miraculous comfort.

So the sadness you see in his eyes is not rejection. He's sad because you've rejected him by not offering him the very thing that has become a barrier in your relationship. If you'd give him your bitterness, you'd be free to draw nearer to him and to feel his miraculous comfort.

To illustrate this further, consider Teresa, a woman I met who carried a great grudge. Her sister, Tasha, had cruelly mistreated their elderly father, putting him into a nursing home that routinely neglected his needs and even barred Teresa from visiting him when he was dying.

Teresa was more than bitter, and when she suddenly ended up in the ICU with a serious infection, she was surprised when she slipped into eternity. As an angel led her away from her body, Teresa found herself face-to-face with Jesus. "I want to go back," she told him. "I don't want to leave my children just yet."

"You can only return if you're willing to forgive Tasha," Jesus told her.

Teresa said, "I am willing," and instantly she found herself back in her body, healed and wondrously free from the bitterness that had formerly consumed her.

The interesting thing is that Jesus did not heal Teresa until she let go of her grudge against her sister. Teresa later confided, "As I stood before Jesus, I had a feeling my bitterness would keep me from spending eternity in God's presence. How glad I am that Jesus helped me, even supplying me with the ability to forgive. All I had to do was agree to forgive my sister, and he did the rest."

Being Right with God Both Now and in Eternity

I long to dwell in heavenly places, not just in the future but now while my feet still touch the earth. I want to come to God with a clean heart, turn to him, and tune my inner ear to his still, small voice. I want to close my eyes and know that though my body still breathes this earth's atmosphere, my spirit breathes the essence of God's very presence. I want to experience all Paul meant when he wrote, "And [God] raised us up together, and made us sit together in the heavenly places in Christ Jesus" (Eph. 2:6 NKJV).

I don't want anything to stop this process, especially my bitterness toward someone else. Therefore, I'm not willing to let anyone, no matter how outrageous their behavior, step between me and God.

Neither did Jesus. For when they hung him on that cruel cross, he prayed, "Father, forgive them, for they do not know what they are doing" (Luke 23:34).

So because I long for more of God's presence, I search my heart, looking for anything that would keep me from having more of God. What I've discovered is that God uses even my difficulties to reveal the condition of my heart. When I discover bitterness, I turn to God and plead, "Help me. Forgive me. Strengthen me as I give even this to you."

Better Emotional and Physical Health

Stephen Stevens said in his book *The Wounded Warrior*, "Some experts estimate that up to 80 percent of health problems can be traced back to one root cause—unforgiveness."[2]

In fact, according to forgiveness researcher Everett Worthington, "Grudges are associated with higher levels of cortisol, a stress hormone that can lead to arterial plaque, which can lead to coronary artery disease."[3]

According to Denise George, in her book *Cultivating a Forgiving Heart*, "Other problems associated with grudge-holding unforgiveness include high blood pressure, insomnia, stomachache, clinching and grinding of teeth, depression, stiff muscles, low energy, anxiety, dizziness, headaches, deep sadness, and so on."[4]

Denise goes on to say, "There is a tiny flower called a saxifrage. Sometimes known as a 'rock-breaker,' it grows secretly in the crevice of strong, solid rocks. It sends down a tiny root in the soil around the rock. Yet as that root begins to grow, it becomes so strong and so powerful, it can literally crack the rock." Denise says, "Given enough time, the small roots of bitterness in our own hearts can grow so strong and so powerful, it can destroy our lives."[5]

Maybe that's why English philosopher and scientist Francis Bacon, born in 1561, said, "This is certain, that a man who studieth revenge keeps his wounds green, which otherwise would heal and do well."[6]

Corrie ten Boom, a Dutch Christian Holocaust survivor who helped many Jews escape the Nazis during World War II, said in her book *Tramp for the Lord*, "Since the end of the war I had had a home in Holland for victims of Nazi brutality. Those who were able to forgive their former enemies were able also to return to the outside world and rebuild their lives, no matter what the physical scars. Those who nursed their bitterness remained invalids. It was as simple and horrible as that."[7]

We would see a lot more physical and emotional healing if we somehow learned how to let go of our bitterness.

It Changes Eternity

I once interviewed Rosemary Trible, the author of *Fear to Freedom*, on a Denver television program. Rosemary described a time in her life, a couple of decades earlier, when she'd been violently raped in her hotel room by a man wearing a ski mask. This man's act of violence stole both her joy and her peace. But over time, though her attacker was never found or arrested, she came to a place where she forgave him, even asking God to send someone who would share the gospel with him.

Years later, Rosemary was in what seemed like a minor fender bender. Not realizing she'd hit her head, she started to drive away but soon felt woozy and pulled over to the side of the road and passed out. There, in a raging snowstorm, Rosemary slipped into a coma. That's when she found herself in a lovely wheat field on the outskirts of heaven. There she was reunited with several dear friends who had already passed over. But as she joyfully chatted with them, the wheat field parted, and a large man she didn't recognize lumbered toward her. She felt anxious and asked, "Who are you?"

The man, humbly and with tears, said, "I am the man who raped you. I would not be here except you forgave me and prayed someone would tell me about Jesus and I would be set free."[8]

The two embraced, and Rosemary was filled with joy, knowing her forgiveness had helped release this man to an eternity with God.

For some of you, the thought of seeing the one who wronged you forgiven and in heaven is the worst thought imaginable. But I know one worse: the thought of the one who wronged you forgiven and in heaven without *you* there.

Please understand, I am not judging you. What I'm trying to say is why allow any barrier between you and the Lord? Let's do all we can to forgive others. And though it may seem impossible to forgive, remember, all things are possible with God (see Mark 10:27).

Whom to Forgive

Poet Henry Wadsworth Longfellow once said, "If we could read the secret history of our enemies, we would find in each person's life sorrow and suffering enough to disarm all hostility."[9]

Perhaps having the inside scoop would, in many cases, make it easier to forgive, but God calls us to forgive whether or not the person in question deserves it. Who are the kinds of people God is calling us to forgive?

- family
- friends
- strangers
- enemies

There are two others on the list who might surprise you:

- yourself
- God

Sometimes the ones you need to forgive include yourself and God.

A few months ago, I felt jealous when some of my friends moved into a more vibrant relationship with God. I felt I couldn't follow them as I would have liked because something was standing in my way. One afternoon, I contemplated my dilemma while walking my dog next to a frozen lake. As I studied the lake's icy surface, God spoke to me. "This is what your heart looks like."

I felt horrified. "My heart is frozen?"

God whispered back, "Only the surface of the lake is frozen. The lake itself is still teeming with life."

I studied the ice that hid the life inside the lake, realizing the ice served as a sort of protective crust.

"Lord," I prayed, "I don't want to shield myself from you. I want you to be able to go fishing in my heart anytime you want." I felt the lake's cold breath brush against my cheeks as I asked, "Can you tell me, Lord, what exactly is this shield I'm holding against you?"

"Disappointment in me and the fact you're mad at yourself."

I instantly understood. My latest prayer battle had not been going the way I'd hoped.

"I'm sorry, Lord," I told him. "I guess I'm upset because I haven't had the breakthrough I was hoping for."

I could feel God's gentle smile as my soul warmed. "Not yet you haven't."

As I stood facing the snow-white lake, I tugged my jacket close and prayed, "Lord, I give you my disappointment and anger. You have my permission to break the ice between us."

It was in that moment that I felt my heart thaw as his love and joy warmed my very being.

What to Forgive

You might be wondering, Is there anything God wouldn't mind if I held on to?

Nope. Just as God forgives us for everything, he wants us to forgive others this same way. The list of things to forgive is a long one and includes abuse, molestation, murder, wrongful death, gossip, betrayal, and lies.

If the condition you are wondering about is not on this list, know that God wants you to put it there.

How to Forgive

The first thing you should know is that forgiveness is a decision. It's not how you feel about someone; it's a choice you make to let go. Corrie ten Boom put it this way: "Forgiveness is an act of the will, and the will can function regardless of the temperature of the heart."[10]

That's exactly what my friend Darla learned the afternoon we talked about her attack. As I held her in my arms, I said, "Darla, God is telling me his name for you is not *Trash*; it's *Precious*. God sees you as beautiful, valuable, and *precious*."

Darla's sobs began to diminish as I continued, "Yes, what Cody did to you was wrong. But it doesn't change God's love for you. When God looks at you, he sees you as pure."

Darla pulled away, her tear-streaked face near mine. "Do you really think so?"

"I do, but I feel you have several people you need to forgive. First, you need to forgive yourself. What happened to you was not your fault. But even if it were, God would still forgive you. But understand, you were not the one who did wrong; you were the victim. Still, I can see you're mad at yourself for even being caught in this situation, aren't you?"

She nodded.

"Can you forgive yourself?"

"I want to."

"Then pray after me." Her soft voice echoed mine. "Lord, I choose to forgive *me*. Give me your strength to forgive myself. I know I was the victim, but I've lived with the shame and guilt of what happened to me all these years. I give my shame and feelings of guilt to you."

Next, I told her, "The next person you need to forgive is God."

She closed her eyes and sobbed, as the question she'd been afraid to face finally surfaced. "Why did God allow this terrible thing to happen to me?"

I placed my hands on her shoulders. "The enemy authored it, but as you know, God allowed it. You're really angry at him for that."

She nodded and studied the floor as hot tears continued to course down her cheeks. "Are you ready to forgive God too?" I asked gently.

She nodded and prayed after me, "Dear Lord, please give me your supernatural strength to forgive you for allowing this attack. I know you didn't author it, but my feelings are hurt that you allowed it. I give you all the anger I've felt toward you. Let this anger no longer be a barrier between us. Please replace it with your peace and help me to know you really do love me."

The flow of her tears ebbed, but I knew we were not yet done. "Now, about the man who attacked you. Darla, I want you to know what he did to you was wrong. He had no right to hurt you. I would never condone his actions and neither would God. Do you understand that?"

She nodded, and I continued, "However, it's not right that this man is still affecting your life today. It's time we gave this man to God so you can move on."

She nodded again. "I'm ready."

Once again, she prayed after me, "Lord, what Cody did to me was wrong. There is no way you or I can justify his brutal attack. But I'm tired of this man being in my daily thoughts. Lord, give me the strength to lay him at your feet and to let go. I now understand that what Cody did to me he also did to you. Therefore, I forgive him because I choose to forgive him. My feelings may not match my choice, but I choose to forgive Cody because it's the only way I can truly be free of him. I forgive him through your power, not mine. Give me the supernatural power to let go. In the name of Jesus, amen."

In that wonderful moment, I saw a miracle as Darla's face reflected peace, and a light in her eyes flickered on. Darla was coming back to life through the power of God and his forgiveness. Later I discovered Darla sitting at the keyboard, playing as she softly worshiped God for the first time in years.

What a transformation, not in Cody but in Darla herself.

Notice that the only thing Darla truly had to do was *choose* to forgive. But that choice was a difficult one.

I was recently speaking to military wives in California, where I spent a session talking about forgiveness. I led the women in a prayer to forgive others then asked them to signal me by quietly pointing to themselves if they were still having trouble forgiving someone.

Though a lot of the women initially let go of their grudges, many signaled they were still stuck. So I asked the group to pray (as can you), "Lord, help me to be *willing to be willing* to forgive." Then later in the morning, we prayed, "Lord, help me to be *willing* to forgive." Then still later, I asked them, "Is the thing you're bitter about worse than what happened to Jesus when he was betrayed, tortured, and crucified for your sins?"

I heard a soft gasp escape from across the room as tears sprang into the eyes of many. I led them in prayer, "Lord, I choose to forgive. Help me to forgive, not through my power but through yours."

Later a woman thanked me for helping her to forgive a difficult situation from her past. She'd been a music teacher at a private school, and through a misunderstanding, she'd been suddenly fired from a job she loved—all because she'd tried to gently guide a not-so-perfectly pitched student away from a degree in music, knowing that college music professors would not be kind or accommodating. But this teacher's words were misconstrued and reported to the school's brass—out of context. The teacher was called to the office, shamed, then fired by the principal. She was given no opportunity to give her side of the story and was required to leave the school grounds immediately. She was not even allowed to say good-bye to or have continued contact with her students.

This dear teacher was devastated and so traumatized that she'd avoided even driving to the town where this had happened, even years later.

But during our group prayer, God set her free. Her eyes were bright with relief as she experienced the miracle of letting go of her grudges and pain through the power of Jesus. How wonderful to see that joy had replaced her shame. Just as God set Darla, Rosemary, me, and this music teacher free, he can set you free too.

How Often Should We Forgive?

Peter was undoubtedly proud of himself when he asked the Master in Matthew 18, "Lord, how often should I forgive someone who sins against me? Seven times?" (v. 21 NLT).

Peter was indeed being generous here, showing his willingness to expand his thinking beyond the three times taught in rabbinical law. How surprised he must have been when Jesus answered, "No, not seven times . . . but seventy times seven!" (v. 22 NLT).

Seventy times seven was a phrase in that day that meant more than 490 times; it actually meant *endless*. In fact, *Barnes' Notes* says "that we are not to limit our forgiveness to any fixed number of times."[11]

So continue to forgive, even the same offense, whenever it comes to mind, for God may continue to lead you to forgive an offense on brand-new levels.

We need to live a lifestyle of continued forgiveness. In other words, as the Lord brings a difficult incident to mind, we should continue to choose to forgive, even when we still feel the pain of the injury.

When we live our lives as forgivers, we forgive, not in our power but in his. This in itself is a miracle. When we can come to this place, we'll further remove the roadblocks to the miracles we long for.

Miraculous Prayer

Dear Lord,

First, I choose to forgive me. Give me your strength to forgive myself. I give my shame and feelings of guilt to you.

Next, give me your supernatural strength to forgive you for allowing _____, not that you authored it, but that you allowed it. I give you my hurt feelings and pain. Please don't let them be a barrier between us. Replace them with your peace and help me to know you really do love me.

Finally, I forgive the one(s) who wronged me. What happened was not right or pleasing to you. But even so, I give _____ to you, God, so I can move on. Lord, give me the strength to lay this person at your feet and to let go. I now understand that what was done to me was also done to you. Therefore, I forgive this person because I choose to forgive. I forgive even if my feelings do not match my choice, because I forgive through your power, not mine.

Give me your supernatural power to let go.

And, Lord, please send someone to the one who wronged me to tell them the good news of your love and forgiveness and truth—so they can spend eternity with you too.

Also, Lord, as I lay my bitterness at your feet, I ask that if my bitterness was preventing my prayer for _____
from being answered, that you would answer it now.
In the name of Jesus, amen.

Scripture to Ponder

(Read aloud.)

Therefore, as God's chosen people, holy and dearly loved, clothe yourselves with compassion, kindness, humility, gentleness and patience. Bear with each other and forgive one another if any of you has a grievance against someone. Forgive as the Lord forgave you. And over all these virtues put on love, which binds them all together in perfect unity.

Colossians 3:12–14

To see a clip of Rosemary Trible, go to www.NeedMiracle Book.com or turn to page 206 for a QR code.

6

What Hinders Our Prayers?

He restores my soul;
> He leads me in the paths of righteousness
> for His name's sake.

Psalm 23:3 NKJV

Because we are seeking miracles, it is a good idea to pray through the following list of things that hinder prayer so that, like David, we can have a "new, clean heart . . . filled with clean thoughts and right desires" (Ps. 51:10 TLB). Such a heart God will hear and bless.

The Hindrance List

Review this list of things that could block your miracle. Then I will show you how to pray to remove the obstacles.

- wrong perspective of God
- not knowing who we are in Christ
- lack of faith and trust
- disappointments
- not asking in the name of Jesus
- grumbling and complaining
- grudges or unforgiveness
- self-will and disobedience
- timidity or fear
- prayerlessness
- unconfessed sin
- not reading the Word
- not standing against the schemes of the enemy
- thanklessness
- not fasting
- not giving

Wrong Perspective of God

It's tempting to believe God is aloof, distant, uncaring, or just plain angry with us. If the enemy has wedged this lie between you and God, let me ask you this: How would your relationship with God be different if this lie didn't exist? Let's replace this lie with truth found in God's Word:

- God loves you so much that he sent his Son to die for you (John 3:16).
- God casts your sins into the depths of the sea (Micah 7:19).
- God forgives you (Rom. 8:1).
- God is near to you as you draw near to him (James 4:8).
- God cares for you (1 Peter 5:7).
- God's presence is with you (1 John 3:19).

The truth is that the majestic God, Creator of the universe, loves you and wants a deeper relationship with you.

Let's pray:

Dear Lord,

I give you my sins in exchange for your forgiveness. Thank you that you cast my sins into the depths of the sea. Thank you that as I turn to you, you draw nearer still. Thank you that you love and care for me. Forgive me for not believing these things about you. I cancel the lie that you're distant, uncaring, and angry with me, for I stand before you forgiven, wearing the righteousness of Christ. You are holy, majestic, and wonderful, and I love and praise you.

In Jesus's name, amen.

Not Knowing Who We Are in Christ

Charles Stanley said in his book *Discovering Your Identity in Christ*, "If we have a faulty self-image—which is having any self-image other than what God says about us—we behave in a way that's contrary to God's highest purposes and plans for our lives."[1]

Through Christ, God sees us as new creations (2 Cor. 5:17); in his eyes, we're forgiven, loved, and cherished. Let's pray:

Dear Lord,

Help me to see myself as you do—forgiven, loved, and cherished—for I am indeed a new creation in Christ. I cancel the lies of the enemy concerning who I am. Lead me into a deeper understanding of my identity in Christ.

In Jesus's name, amen.

Lack of Faith and Trust

Is God able?

Yes! Paul, in fact, wrote a letter to the church in Ephesus, saying, "Now to him who is able to do immeasurably more than all we ask or imagine, according to his power that is at work within us" (Eph. 3:20).

One dad discovered this truth for himself. You see, his son was demon possessed, and even Jesus's disciples were unable to cast out the evil spirit. But when the spirit saw Jesus, it immediately threw the boy into a convulsion. Mark 9 continues the story:

> Jesus asked the boy's father, "How long has he been like this?"
>
> "From childhood," he answered. "It has often thrown him into fire or water to kill him. But if you can do anything, take pity on us and help us."
>
> "'If you can'?" said Jesus. "Everything is possible for one who believes."
>
> Immediately the boy's father exclaimed, "I do believe; help me overcome my unbelief!" . . .
>
> [Jesus] rebuked the impure spirit. "You deaf and mute spirit," he said, "I command you, come out of him and never enter him again."
>
> The spirit shrieked, convulsed him violently and came out. The boy looked so much like a corpse that many said, "He's dead." But Jesus took him by the hand and lifted him to his feet, and he stood up. (vv. 21–27)

Jesus healed the boy despite his dad's lack of faith, demonstrated by his saying, "If you *can*," instead of, "If you *will*."

But as soon as this father realized his mistake, he professed his faith: "I believe." Then he asked for even more faith: "Help my unbelief." So even the dad's faith was a gift from God.

But get this. For the first few moments after Jesus prayed, the boy appeared to be dead. Can you imagine the doubt the father must have felt?

Personally, I think this is good news for those of us who have gotten a bad report or for those of us who continue to pray or believe when our situation seems hopeless. Through Christ and his power, those things that seem dead can be very much alive. Pray this:

> Dear Lord,
> I know you "can," so I choose to trust you, even when I cannot see what you're doing. I choose to look not at the bad report but to you.
> In Jesus's name, amen.

Disappointments

Sometimes we get so caught up in our own disappointments that we fail to see Jesus. That's exactly what happened to two of Jesus's disciples after his death. Oh sure, they had been there when the women had come from the garden tomb with a wild story that Jesus had risen from the dead. But these two didn't believe a word of it.

Now, as they walked down the road together, Jesus himself caught up with them. But did they recognize him? No. They were too focused on their disappointment to see the miracle of his presence, never mind that all the while he walked with them he explained the Scriptures concerning himself. He even said, "How foolish you are, and how slow to believe all that the prophets have spoken! Did not the Messiah have to suffer these things and then enter his glory?" (Luke 24:25–26).

It wasn't until the dinner hour when Jesus broke bread with them that they were able to take their eyes off their disappointment long enough to see their resurrected Lord sitting before them. They had so wallowed in self-pity that they had failed to see that Jesus had been with them the entire afternoon.

The same thing happens to us. When we're faced with disappointment, we sometimes focus on the disappointment itself rather than on the fact that Jesus is walking us through the disappointment.

I recently talked to a group of faithful employees of a powerful ministry that was closing due to a scandal in leadership. I told the employees and volunteers, "I've been in ministry for a couple of decades now, and there have been times I've had great disappointments. But you can't let those disappointments stop you from continuing your faith walk with God. For God is in the business of flipping disappointments into victories."

One precious woman asked, "You mean like in the story of Joseph? What the enemy meant for evil, God meant for good?"

"Exactly. Now that this ministry has closed, God is freeing you to continue in your journey to new areas of service and victory you would not have discovered if you'd never been disappointed."

Later, we called each employee and volunteer to the front of the room to present them with a certificate thanking them for their faithful service. It was a well-deserved moment that reminded them that what they had done for the kingdom *had* made a difference.

If you've ever been tripped up by disappointment, I want to present you with a certificate as well. Please read the following as if it had your name on it, because it does:

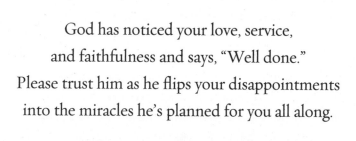

God has noticed your love, service,
and faithfulness and says, "Well done."
Please trust him as he flips your disappointments
into the miracles he's planned for you all along.

Amen to that! Let's pray:

> *Dear Lord,*
> *Forgive me when I've been more focused on disappointments*
> *than on you. Help me to realize, despite my disappointments,*
> *that you are with me. Help me to have faith to believe. Flip my*
> *disappointments into miracles.*
> *In Jesus's name, amen.*

Not Asking in the Name of Jesus

A friend pulled me aside and asked, "Why do you pray in Jesus's name?"

I answered, "Jesus himself commanded us to do so when he said, 'And I will do whatever you ask in my name, so that the Father may be glorified in the Son. You may ask me for anything in my name, and I will do it' (John 14:13–14)."

In other words, Jesus is the door to God (John 14:6). We need to enter that door whenever we want to ask anything of God. Let's pray:

> *Dear God,*
> *Thank you that I can come to you in the power of the name*
> *of your Son, Jesus. I ask for the following prayer request:*
>
> _____.
>
> *In Jesus's name, amen.*

Grumbling and Complaining

I've always found it interesting that though God didn't write, "Do not grumble or complain" as his eleventh commandment, he takes our grumbling and complaining personally. In fact, he got so sick of hearing the wandering Israelites complain about the food he provided in the desert that he sent poisonous snakes to bite them.

Our grumbling bothers God because it proves we've failed to see or appreciate his loving provision.

Let's pray:

> Dear Lord,
> Please forgive me for grumbling and complaining about my circumstances. Help me not to overlook your provision but to trust in you. Thank you for all you have done for me.
> In Jesus's name, amen.

Grudges or Unforgiveness

If this area continues to be a stumbling block for you, go back to chapter 5 and reread the prayers. Don't be discouraged. Sometimes we have to pray these prayers repeatedly before we get the emotional breakthrough we need. But in the meantime pray:

> Dear Lord,
> Help me to live a lifestyle where I continue to choose to forgive, not through my power, but through yours.
> In Jesus's name, amen.

Self-Will and Disobedience

Is it important to God that we follow his will? Ask King Saul, a man God favored until he disobeyed God's instruction and brought home forbidden spoils of war. His disobedience was in fact the very reason God turned his face from Saul to David.

Don't let disobedience and self-will hinder answers to prayer. As 1 John 5:14 says, "This is the confidence we have in approaching God: that if we ask anything according to his will, he hears us."

> *Dear Lord,*
> *Give me wisdom and discernment to hear your voice, know your will, and then obey it. Remind me of the thing you have told me to do and guide me as I do it. Forgive me when I fail, and give me the strength to obey you now.*
> *In Jesus's name, amen.*

Timidity or Fear

I was in a small prayer circle when one of my friends asked, "Linda, can you tell me about your first memory of being afraid?"

I replied, "This might sound silly, but I remember myself as a five-year-old staring at the white organza curtains in my bedroom. I felt certain the big bad wolf actually *lived* in my curtains.

"At night, after my mother would read me a story about the big bad wolf, I'd lie in bed and stare at my curtains, imagining what would happen if this terrible creature actually stepped into my room."

I laughed at the memory, but Dianna said, "How did it make you feel to think your life was so uncertain, to think a frightening wolf could enter your world at any moment?"

I inwardly winced as I realized I often entertained fearful thoughts of imagined dangers.

Dianna asked, "Would you like to be set free from constant fear?"

"I would like that," I said.

Dianna led me in a prayer, a prayer you too can pray:

> *Dear Lord,*
> *There is nothing that can happen to me that you do not already have in your plan book for my life. There is nothing*

*that can happen to me that will take me out of your will. Even
if the enemy does attack, you will use whatever circumstance
happens as the seed of the miracles you have planned for me
since the beginning of time. I do not have to be afraid, for you
are with me, and the bottom line is this: I trust you with every
moment of my life.*

In Jesus's name, amen.

Live as though you're not afraid of the future, because God
is there with a plan.

Prayerlessness

It's amazing how many of us don't pray on a regular basis.
In fact, James 4:2 says, "You desire but do not have, so you kill.
You covet but you cannot get what you want, so you quarrel and
fight. You do not have because you do not ask God."

But do we really have to ask? After all, isn't God a mind
reader?

God certainly knows our minds, but he's certainly not a magic
genie ready to perform at our every whim. One of the main reasons God answers prayer is that he's after a deeper relationship
with us. When we seek him with our whole heart, he notices
and responds with love.

So pray—daily, hourly, or by the minute, even if it's just small
prayers such as, "Lord, I just wanted to let you know I love you,"
or, "Help Jenny to do well on her test today."

But beyond that, I recommend you set aside time daily to talk
to God and to tell him what is on your heart.

In addition, I recommend you write down your prayer requests
as petitions, as mentioned in Philippians 4:6. "Do not be anxious
about anything, but in every situation, by prayer and petition,
with thanksgiving, present your requests to God."

To create my written petitions, I write Philippians 4:6 at the top of a blank page, then beneath it I write, "This is my petition to the Lord God of the universe. With prayer and thanksgiving, I petition God to:"

Next, I list my requests. For example, here are a few things from my personal list:

1. help me hear his voice clearly and have better discernment
2. reach millions of people for Christ
3. lower my cholesterol
4. help me lose twenty-five pounds
5. help me write an anointed book about miracles

When I finish writing my list, I sign and date it, then add it to my prayer notebook, which I've filled with petitions for myself, my ministries, and my family members. It's fun to go back to see how God has answered my petitions with miracles. To print out a copy of a blank prayer petition to use yourself, go to www. NeedMiracleBook.com or turn to page 206 for a QR code.

But regardless of whether you create written petitions, keep going to God with both silent and spoken prayer. E. M. Bounds once said, "Prayer puts God's work in his hands and keeps it there."[2] Let's pray:

> *Dear Lord,*
>
> *Forgive me for my prayerlessness. Constantly remind me that you are waiting for my requests, comments, and thoughts. In fact, I'd like to spend some time with you right now regarding [tell him what's on your heart].*
>
> *In Jesus's name, amen.*

Unconfessed Sin

This is one we don't like to talk about much, but Psalm 66:18–20 makes it clear: "If I had not confessed the sin in my heart, the Lord would not have listened. But God did listen! He paid attention to my prayer. Praise God, who did not ignore my prayer or withdraw his unfailing love from me" (NLT).

If we expect God to hear us, we must confess (and also turn away from) the sin in our hearts. Let's pray:

> Dear Lord,
> Please forgive me for the sins I've committed [list them], as well as the sins I've been pondering in my heart [list them]. I choose to turn away from them in your supernatural strength.
> Also, please hear my prayers. I ask you for _____.
> Thank you that you'll not ignore my prayer.
> In Jesus's name, amen.

Not Reading the Word

Joshua 1:8 is a command attached to a promise: "Keep this Book of the Law always on your lips; meditate on it day and night, so that you may be careful to do everything written in it. Then you will be prosperous and successful."

When we thank God, we're reminding ourselves that his presence is with us.

If you need wisdom, you must pick up your Bible and read, for reading the Word is the fastest way to find wisdom and the best way to hear God's voice. If you don't know where to start, might I suggest John, James, the Psalms, or even Proverbs? Pray this:

> Dear Lord,
> Please forgive me for not making time to read your Word.
> I choose to set aside time daily so that you can speak to me.
> In Jesus's name, amen.

Not Standing against the Schemes of the Enemy

The next couple of chapters will cover this.

Thanklessness

Psalm 95 gives God a shout out: "Let us come to him with thanksgiving. Let us sing psalms of praise to him" (v. 2 NLT).

When we thank God, we're reminding ourselves that his presence is with us.

Andrew Murray once said, "Thanksgiving will draw our hearts out to God and keep us engaged with Him; it will take our attention from ourselves and give the Spirit room in our hearts."[3]

Pray this:

> Dear Lord,
> Please forgive me for the times I've forgotten to thank you, for despite my troubles, you have blessed me with [list blessings]. Thank you so much for being my God, my guide, and my champion.
> In Jesus's name, amen.

Not Fasting

Elmer L. Towns said in his book *The Beginners' Guide to Fasting*, "When you can't get an answer to prayer, even though you have prayed continually, try fasting with your prayer. Fasting demonstrates your sincerity to God. . . . When you give up food—that which is enjoyable and necessary—you get God's attention."[4]

Before you try fasting, do a little research to find the best fast for you. As for me, I usually go on a partial fast, taking sugar, wheat, and caffeine out of my diet for a couple of weeks.

A friend of mine told me that when her son was serving in the military in Iraq, she and her husband often fasted and prayed continually for his safety. Joyce said, "It was one of the sweetest times with both the Lord and my husband. How Rob and I rejoiced when our son returned home safe and sound."

> *Dear Lord,*
> *Please lead me in this area. Teach me how to deny myself so that I can better follow you.*
> *In Jesus's name, amen.*

Not Giving

Kenneth Boa wrote in his book *Conformed to His Image*, "We must come to grips with the fact that everything we have in this world belongs to God and is only on loan to us. This includes not only our money and possessions but also our families, careers, and plans for the future."[5]

When trying to explain why our money (and how we handle it) is so important to God, Boa points out, "Money is a good servant but a bad master. If we follow the world's wisdom, money will dominate us, but if we submit to the 'wisdom from above' (James 3:17), money will serve us as we use it to serve God and others."[6]

It's better to give than to keep. Jesus said in Luke 6:38, "For if you give, you will get! Your gift will return to you in full and overflowing measure, pressed down, shaken together to make room for more, and running over. Whatever measure you use to give—large or small—will be used to measure what is given back to you" (TLB).

This is a spiritual principle: we give and God provides. Unfortunately, this principle has often been exploited by those who would tell you, "Name it, pay me, and claim it."

It may be better, if you want to respond to God's call to give, to bypass the "name it and pay me" bunch and instead care for orphans and widows (James 1:26–27) and support your local church. But how much should we give?

Passages in the Old Testament suggest we should give God a tenth of all we have (Lev. 27:32). Before you complain that this is too high a price in this economy, try it and see if God will not meet you there. Even if your hand trembles when you drop your hard-earned cash in the offering plate, give it with joy. As you give, God will begin to prove himself to you, and you'll soon discover you can't outgive God.

Let me warn you, however, not to "give" to "get." Give instead to show your love for the Lord, and become a "cheerful giver" (2 Cor. 9:6).

Dear Lord,
Please forgive me for my disobedience in this area and for my secret motivation of giving to get. Instruct me on how to give, and give me the ability to give with cheer, out of my love for you.
In Jesus's name, amen.

It Really Is about Trusting God

Can you imagine what a disaster it would be if God answered our *exact* prayers instead of the *intent* of our prayers?

In *Finding the Heart's True Home*, Richard J. Foster said:

Many times in our shortsightedness we ask for things that are not in our best interests. At other times the answers to our prayers will be detrimental to others, or mean the refusal of their prayers, or both. Then there are times when our prayers are simply self-contradictory, a "grant me patience quickly" kind of prayer. And finally, sometimes our prayers, if answered, would do us in. We're simply not yet prepared for what we have asked.

In such cases, and many others like them, it is God's grace and mercy that prevent our prayers from being answered. God withholds his gifts from us for our good. We could not handle what might come if our requests were granted. So we must thank God that many of our prayers go unanswered. C. S. Lewis writes, "If God had granted all the silly prayers I've made in my life, where would I be now?"[7]

> *Sometimes God says no because he is simply trying to protect us.*

But in addition to making unwise requests, we also may not always be in tune with God's responses. Foster explains: "Many times our prayers are indeed answered, but we lack the eyes to see it."[8]

It all boils down to trusting God. Scottish theologian P. T. Forsyth once said, "We shall come one day to a heaven where we shall gratefully know God's greatest refusals were sometimes the true answers to our truest prayers."[9]

You really can trust God. Sometimes God says no because he is simply trying to protect us.

Miraculous Prayer

Go back and pray all the prayers in this chapter as needed.

Scripture to Ponder

(Read aloud.)

> Blessed is the one… whose delight is in the law of the
> LORD,
> and who meditates on his law day and night.
> That person is like a tree planted by streams of water,
> which yields its fruit in season

and whose leaf does not wither—
whatever they do prospers.

Psalm 1:1–3

To see Linda's interview, go to www.NeedMiracleBook.com or turn to page 206 for a QR code.

7

Fighting the Enemy

Fight the good fight of the faith.

1 Timothy 6:12

If you've ever wondered if the Bible talks about spiritual warfare, turn to Matthew 6 and read the Lord's Prayer. There in the thirteenth verse Jesus taught us to pray, "Deliver us from evil" (KJV).

I'm glad Jesus taught us this, because as you might have noticed, evil is out there and can impact us, our families, and our loved ones. So maybe it's a good idea to spend some time praying, "Lord, deliver us from evil," as part of our miracle quest.

But some of you may be wondering, *Deliver me? If God can flip any circumstance into good, why shouldn't I rush headlong into trouble?*

Well, you're right about one thing. God can flip any circumstance. But why invite trouble, especially when Jesus said in

101

John 10:10, "The thief comes only to steal and kill and destroy; I came that they may have life, and have it abundantly" (NASB).

So if you're like me, you'll want to shut that thief out and choose abundant life. In fact, I'll be the first to admit that when I find myself in trouble, I waste no time calling out to God. However, I'm happy to know that he can use any of my troubles for good (Gen. 50:20; Rom. 8:28).

You should never feel guilty for calling out to God when things go wrong. Many a biblical great has made that call, including Job. As we've discussed, Job was a God-fearing man who had several tragedies hit him within an hour. We can trace the root cause of Job's woes to Satan's design. But Job sought God, and in the end, God restored two times what Job had lost. God turned Job's life around even though Job believed, at least for a time, that God was ignoring him.

> *You should never feel guilty for calling out to God when things go wrong.*

So if Satan had authority—with God's permission—over Job, shouldn't we be afraid of Satan?

No. Satan has authority over us only when God allows him to test us, when we give Satan authority over us through our own sin, or when we do not know how to fight against him.

But do we have the authority to fight Satan?

Yes. In fact, Jesus said in Luke 10:18–20, "I saw Satan fall like lightning from heaven. I have given you authority to trample on snakes and scorpions and to overcome all the power of the enemy; nothing will harm you. However, do not rejoice that the spirits submit to you, but rejoice that your names are written in heaven."

It's often said that Jesus meant this saying only for the seventy disciples he sent to heal the sick and cast out demons. But when we consider that this viewpoint has only been around for the past one hundred years *and* that "Jesus Christ is the same yesterday, today, and forever" (Heb. 13:8 NKJV), then perhaps we should also consider that the same authority granted to the seventy may also be meant for us. In fact, Colossians 2:9–10 reminds us, "For in Christ all the fullness of the Deity lives in bodily form, and in Christ you have been brought to fullness. He is the head over every power and authority." Therefore, I like to pray in his will in the authority Jesus has given me through his name (Acts 16:18) and shed blood (Col. 1:19–20). In other words, I'm praying in the power and authority of Jesus, not mine. Also, in that authority, I can cast out, cancel, or eject the works of the enemy because I know that Jesus came to destroy the works of the enemy (1 John 3:8).

However, we have to remember that God (not we ourselves or even Satan) is the one with the final say. And because God is sovereign, he may indeed allow the enemy to test us to build our faith or to allow for God's glory and goodness to come as a result of our trial. Consider the words of Jesus in Revelation 2:10: "Do not be afraid of what you are about to suffer. I tell you, the devil will put some of you in prison to test you, and you will suffer persecution for ten days. Be faithful, even to the point of death, and I will give you life as your victor's crown."

It appears that the Lord will allow Satan to test us. But this testing can be counted for joy. James 1:2–4 says, "My brethren, count it all joy when you fall into various trials, knowing that the testing of your faith produces patience. But let patience have its perfect work, that you may be perfect and complete, lacking nothing" (NKJV).

Confused? Look at it this way. Though we have been set free, there are still battles we must fight. In those battles, there are times we can take complete authority over the enemy through the power of Christ, but there are other times God allows the enemy to test us (within limits [Job 1:12]) to accomplish the perfecting of our faith.

So how are we supposed to know when we should fight Satan or when we must submit to the test? Well, we let God decide by remembering to pray in his will. Then we wait on the leading of the Holy Spirit. If he leads us to fight, we fight through the power of God and the authority of the name and blood of Jesus, but if he leads us to be tested, we endure the test *also* through the power of God and the authority of the name and blood of Jesus.

But regardless of whether we fight the enemy or we wait on God through a test, we come to God with a decision to trust him, praising him that he is with us and then resting in his peace.

Fighting the Enemy

But when God's Word and Spirit call us to fight, what do we do?

First, we should understand that we're in a battle. Paul, in his letter to the Ephesians, put it this way: "For our struggle is not against flesh and blood, but against the rulers, against the authorities, against the powers of this dark world and against the spiritual forces of evil in the heavenly realms" (6:12).

In 2 Kings 6, we get an interesting glimpse into these heavenly realms. When the king of Syria was at war with Israel, Elisha the prophet was able to thwart his plans by warning the king of Israel of the Syrians' plans. Finally, the Syrian king had enough of God's tattletale and sent his army to the city of Dothan to capture Elisha.

That morning, when the young man who served Elisha stepped out of his tent, he was shocked to see the Syrian army with their chariots and horses surrounding his city. We can read the passage to see what happened next.

"Alas, my master, what shall we do now?" he cried out to Elisha.

"Don't be afraid!" Elisha told him. "For our army is bigger than theirs!"

Then Elisha prayed, "Lord, open his eyes and let him see!" And the Lord opened the young man's eyes so that he could see horses of fire and chariots of fire everywhere upon the mountain! (15–17 TLB)

What a moment, a moment that causes me to wonder what kind of warfare or warriors average praying Christians would see if the Lord opened their eyes to see into the unseen.

The unseen battle rages on. Not long ago I was speaking to a group of evangelical pastors' wives when I mentioned how the enemy was at work in our churches. One of the wives raised her hand. "You're right, Linda. It's heartbreaking to see what's happening in my own church with attacks on my husband. Plus, so many members have a sort of cold love; it mimics the love of Christ, but it's anything but. Please tell me, tell us, how to pray against these assaults."

I answered, "We need to do warfare to break the spirit of religion, strife, deception, and cold love over our churches."

"Could you lead us in a prayer to show us how?"

I prayed as these dear women prayed with me:

Dear Lord,

We come to you on behalf of our church. First, we repent for being caught up in the spirit of religion, strife, deception, unbelief, and cold love. Please forgive us. We choose to turn from these sins. Give us your power to both forgive and reconcile with those we have hurt as well as those who have hurt us.

Next, we ask you to deliver our church from all evil. We resist the enemy so that he will flee. Jesus came to destroy the works of the enemy, so we call upon God's power, in the authority of the name and blood of Jesus, to cancel the enemy's plans as well as to annul, cast out, and expel the spirit of religion, strife, deception, and cold love in our church.

Lord, we ask you to replace these evil spirits, sins, and issues with your love and power to forgive and reconcile. As your Word tells us, Jesus is standing at the door knocking, so we invite the Son, as well as the Father and the Holy Spirit, to come in and to have an even stronger presence in our church than ever before. Jesus, please come in and dine and fellowship with us. Teach us how to have a deeper relationship with you. May your joy be our strength. May your grace and truth set us free.

In Jesus's name, amen.

The pastors' wives were excited to learn how to pray this kind of prayer, and now you can pray this prayer for your own church. In fact, why not invite a team of people to pray this prayer with you weekly or daily. Watch and see God move your church to revival. Go to www.NeedMiracleBook.com or turn to page 206 for a QR code for a copy of this prayer to send or email to your praying friends, asking them to pray it on behalf of your church.

I'm going to give you the outline of this prayer and the strategy behind it so you can pray a warfare prayer in other situations.

- "I come to you on behalf of [person or group]."—Tell God for whom you are praying.
- "First, I repent of these sins of [anger, strife, pride, bitterness, grief, trauma, spiritual blindness, etc.]."—This is key! If you humble yourself and repent of the issue(s) you've named, you will shut the door you may have inadvertently opened to the enemy in these areas.
- "Please forgive me as I forgive those who have sinned against me."—You are asking for forgiveness as you forgive others.

This act of forgiveness will continue to free you from the enemy's schemes.

- "Next, I ask you to deliver [name person or situation] from all evil. I resist the enemy so that he will flee (James 4:7). Jesus came to destroy the works of the enemy, so I call upon God's power, in the authority of the name and blood of Jesus, to cancel the enemy's plans as well as to annul, cast out, and expel [name spirits] in [name person(s) or situation]."—You do not have the authority to cancel, annul, cast out, or expel these spirits or their plans on your own but only through the mighty name and blood of Jesus. Use that authority. We know it's never God's will to allow these sins or spirits into our lives. But in the meantime, remember to follow Jesus's model in the Lord's Prayer and simply ask the Lord to deliver you from all evil (Matt. 6:13).

Also, note that when we pray against those in Satan's camp, we resist the works of the enemy with the confidence of who we are in Jesus Christ, his authority on which we stand, as well as the Bible's assurance of Satan's defeat. We may be challenged, but the Holy Spirit will help us stand strong.

So in other words, when you pray against the enemy's plans and works (which happen to be the "worker bee" demons' orders), you are actually sending confusion into the enemy's camp, a very effective warfare strategy.

- "Lord, I ask you to replace these evil spirits, sins, and issues with [your love and power to forgive and reconcile, etc.]."—As you resist the devil with prayer, God's power will cause the enemy to flee. Fill the void left behind by the enemy's retreat with forgiveness, love, joy, peace, or some other fruit of the Spirit. For example, pray for "your joy instead of sorrow," "your peace instead of fear," "your humility instead of pride," etc.

- "I invite you, Lord God, your Son, and the Holy Spirit to come into this situation and to have a deeper relationship with me."—When you take your situation to God, you will find God is bigger still. Welcome God's presence into the situation, not because he's not there already but because you need to be reminded that he is there. Then you can offer God more access, faith, and trust regarding the problem. Next, seek to fellowship with him even in the midst of your problem, because that's where you will find an even greater intimacy with him.
- "May your joy be my strength."—God's joy and strength are additional tools you can use to overcome difficulties.
- "May your grace and truth set me free."—I pray for God's grace whenever I can. Also, note that there could be other sins or demonic influences still lurking in the situation in question. By asking for God's truth, you are asking God to reveal all other lies or the existence of additional evil spirits so you can be set free. You are also asking for truth to open the eyes of all involved in the situation, for spiritual blindness can hold individuals, churches, cities, or even governments in bondage. May we all be set free from spiritual blindness (Eph. 4:17–19).
- "In Jesus's name, amen."—Always, always pray in the name of Jesus.

I hope you better understand both the why and the how of spiritual warfare prayers. But you might ask, "Do we really have the power and the authority to pray such prayers?"

Paul thought so. He told his friends in Ephesus:

I also pray that you will understand the incredible greatness of God's power for us who believe him. This is the same mighty power that raised Christ from the dead and seated him in the place of honor at God's right hand in the heavenly realms. Now he is far above any ruler or authority or power or leader or anything else—not only in this world but also in the world to come. God has put all things under the authority of Christ and has made him head over all things for the benefit of the church. And the church is his body; it is made full and complete by Christ, who fills all things everywhere with himself. (Eph. 1:19–23 NLT)

In other words, Jesus is above Satan and all his spiritual wickedness in high places. Therefore, when we pray through the name and authority of Jesus, our prayers have access to more power than we could ever imagine.

The Set Free Prayer

I met a woman who had adopted a child from Haiti. "I am the second adoptive mother of my son," the woman explained. "You see, he was the biological son of a voodoo priest. He had a lot of issues, physical and behavioral problems related to his occultic past. His first adoptive mother couldn't handle him, and I have to admit, his problems were so severe I wasn't sure I could either. But a friend of mine sent me a warfare prayer to break the spiritual strongholds on my son. Since I've started praying it, my son has calmed down. He's peaceful and happy, and things are going very well for him. I attribute the change in my son to this prayer I continue to pray over him daily."

This story got my attention, especially because the young boy sat by her side with a peaceful smile throughout the worship and prayer service we were attending. His countenance was proof enough to convince me he'd been transformed. So I requested a copy of this set free prayer and spent the next several months studying and revising it. In fact, I was so impressed with what I learned by praying it, I want to teach it to you as we continue studying spiritual warfare as a way to find the miracles we long for.

The set free prayer is a good addition to the first warfare prayer that we covered and will help you break through any remaining strongholds in your life. I recommend you pray it, or at least sections of it, daily or until the Lord releases you. Its comprehensive nature will help you combat forces, spirits, strongholds, and issues you may not have yet recognized are in your situation. For example, one woman I led in this prayer suddenly realized she'd been hounded by a spirit of depression for years. When she unmasked it, she was able to cancel its assignment in the power of the name and blood of Jesus. She is now joyfully free of her former depression which, until she had prayed through the set free prayer, had seemed like a normal part of her life.

You too may be surprised at what you could be set free from, so pray this prayer whenever God puts it on your heart. You can practice intercession as you stand, through God's power, against evil forces that have come against you as well as anyone you have in your sphere of influence. You can use your legal authority to pray over your children, spouse, parents, employees, as well as any others who grant you permission. You can pray it over any others too, but these results may be slower to appear. But pray anyway as God leads.

What is legal authority?

The spirit world does things in order. It's easier, for example, to pray a spiritual warfare prayer over a person who repents and is in agreement with your prayers than over a person who is unrepentant and who does not agree with your prayers. In the second case, you can pray anyway, but you will probably be met with more spiritual resistance from the enemy *unless* God has put you in a position of authority over this person. In other words, if this disagreeing person is your own child, you have more legal rights or authority (in the spirit realm) to pray over them than you would over an unrepentant person you meet on the street corner. You can still pray for the person on the street corner, but it may take more time and effort to pray through the spiritual resistance you will likely encounter, unless God sovereignly does a great work. The reason is that the enemy is reluctant to give up someone who is in agreement with their sin or addiction. However, continued prayers can make a difference, and many people are free today because someone was committed to praying for them, no matter how long it took.

But you may ask, "Has God really given us the right to go into spiritual warfare?" Let's consider 2 Corinthians 10:4–5, which says, "For the weapons of our warfare are not carnal but mighty in God for pulling down strongholds, casting down arguments and every high thing that exalts itself against the knowledge of God, bringing every thought into captivity to the obedience of Christ" (NKJV).

So as you pray the spiritual warfare prayer below, feel free to add any issues or concerns not already included. Also, be sure to continue to pray the sections significant to you. Please note that the first section is broken into categories, including:

- issues—This includes all issues, sins, and difficulties.
- words used against you—Words and curses can create bondages and entanglements that can be broken by the mighty name of Jesus.
- evil weapons—This includes any weapon the enemy or those who serve him may have used or are using against you. All spells and powers from voodoo or witchcraft can be broken in Jesus's name.
- the worship of ungodly forces—You need to take yourself out from under any spiritual authority of the enemy, especially if you have purposely or inadvertently worshiped or

messed with a deity, spirit, or principality other than God. You can break any ungodly authority over you through the mighty name of Jesus.

- all evil influences of false religion or occultic leaders and practitioners—If a practitioner of the occult should try to influence, harass, or harm you, with or without your knowledge, you can annul their power and authority over you through the name of Jesus.
- all ungodly addictions—Addictions can be broken in the power of God, through Jesus.
- your own involvement, covenants, curses, and oaths—You can break any connection between you and your past involvement with the occult through the power of the name of Jesus.
- personal, family, as well as generational curses—All curses that are set to harm you and your family members can be broken through the mighty name of Jesus.

The Set Free Prayer Part 1

Dear Lord,

It is your will for me to be set free from any sin, spiritual condition, attack, or strategy of the enemy that hinders me or [name the person] from a deeper walk and ministry with and through you. Jesus said in John 8:32, "And ye shall know the truth, and the truth shall make you free" (KJV). Lord, I choose to know your truth and the freedom you have made possible for me and [name the person] through the work and shed blood of Jesus.

First, I ask you to forgive me of my sin, through the death and resurrection of Jesus. Next, Lord, please cover me, my family, and [name the person] with the blood of Jesus as you deliver us from evil. Now, in the authority and power of the name and blood of Jesus, I ask you to lead me in the power and counsel of the Holy Spirit so I can move against the strategies of the enemy in the authority of Christ. In addition, I ask you to cleanse me from all unrighteousness as I repent and turn from cooperating with the plans of the enemy. Because Jesus came to destroy the works of the devil, through the authority and power of the name and blood of Jesus, I cancel, annul, sever, cast out, and eject from me, my family, and [name the person] all of the enemy's assignments, attacks, blindness, connections, covenants, curses, deception, influences, involvement, lies, plans, strategies, strongholds, targeting, or ties regarding:

- *Issues or spirits of abandonment, abortion, abuse, accidents, anger, antichrist, cancer, confusion, control, death, deceit, delusions, depression, destruction, discord, disunity, divorce, envy, exhaustion, false gifts or manifestations, fear, greed, grief, grumbling, guilt, hate, jealousy, lies, loss, mental attacks, illness or dementias, misconceptions, misdirection, misunderstandings, murder, negativity, offense, overeating, physical ailments or attacks, pornography, pride, rebellion, self-destruction, self-hate, self-pity, selfishness, shame, sickness, sin, spiritual blindness, stress, strife, suicide, theft, timidity, tragedies, trauma, unbelief, ungodly soul-ties, unforgiveness, and wrath.*

- *All evil, negative, or ungodly words and pronouncements, including complaints; condemnation; curses; death wishes (spoken or unspoken); discouragements; and false criticisms, judgments, prophecies, predictions, and teachings. Also, all gossip, insults, lies, lyrics, murmuring, ridicule, slander, and prayers or words not inspired, directed, or willed by God or his Holy Spirit.*

113

- *All evil weapons used by or against me and my family, including bewitchments, candle burning, ceremonies, charms, curses, demonic media (including but not limited to computer games, books, internet, movies, music, pornography, TV, websites), fetishes, fortune-telling, hexes, horoscopes, hypnoses, incantations, incense, jinxes, magic, mind control, music, nightmares, oaths, Ouija boards, pacts, pain, palm reading, potions, psychic power or spells, sleeplessness, sorcery, soul force, tarot cards, ungodly forces, ungodly prayers, vexes, voodoo, warfare, and witchcraft.*
- *The worship or influence of all ungodly spiritual forces, including angel or demon worship; Apollyon; Baal; false religions; Isis; Jezebel; nature-, creation-, or self-worship; the occult; Pele; Satan worship; secret (or not so secret) societies or cults that worship Babylonian, Egyptian, ancient Greek, or other false gods, goddesses, principalities, and wickedness.*
- *All evil influences of false religion or occultic leaders and practitioners, including counterfeit Christians, Satanists, shamans, voodoo priests, warlocks, witch doctors, witches, wizards, and other false religious practitioners.*
- *All ungodly addictions, including alcohol; cigarettes or any kind of inhalable; computer games; cutting; drugs; eating disorders; gambling; internet; pornography; satanic or ungodly music; sexual conquests, encounters, imaginations, or thoughts; and television or other media.*
- *My own involvement or connections with, covenants with, curses, and oaths to any covens, cults, or ungodly entities, including deities, demons, fraternities, gods, lodges, orders, organizations, principalities, religions, sororities, or spiritual forces, including Satan and other wickedness.*

- *Personal, family, and generational curses, as well as curses created against me or my family or by my sins or the sins of my family or ancestors.*

In Jesus's name, amen.

The Set Free Prayer Part 2

Part 1 of this prayer certainly covers a lot of territory the enemy would like to hang on to. But pray this prayer daily and watch as God begins to give you the breakthroughs you need. It may seem like a lot of time and work, but imagine how much time you will save if your life and the lives of your friends and family members come into God's order because you were willing to pray.

The second part of the set free prayer extends forgiveness to others and breaks curses, judgments, or lies, spoken accidently or not, against others. It's a way to pray into the spiritual principle that when we set others free, God will set us free.

Dear Lord,

Through the power of the Lord Jesus himself, I forgive all people who have come against me in any way, who have betrayed, cursed, deceived, despitefully used, hated, hurt, falsely judged, lied about, believed a lie about, or rejected me or stolen from me. I give you my anger, bitterness, grief, hate, hurt, trauma, and wounds so that the enemy will not be able to use anger, bitterness, grief, hate, hurt, trauma, or wounds as a stronghold or weapon against me or others. In the power and authority of the name and blood of Jesus, I break any curses, judgments, or lies I've thought and/or spoken against others accidently or not.

In Jesus's name, amen.

The Set Free Prayer Part 3

The third part of this prayer may need to be prayed only on occasion. It's designed to cover any time we may have attacked the enemy with the weapon of our own pride. For example, if you've ever shaken your fist at Satan and said, "I'm a child of the King. I'm not afraid of you, so give me your best shot," you most likely said it in pride.

While it's true you are a child of the King, it's also true you do not want to do anything out of order, especially when you are in a spiritual battle. Coming at a being who rebelled against God because of his own pride, with pride, is out of order. Such tactics will only inflame the enemy and possibly put you under his legal authority to torment you. Therefore, it's important to use the strategy of humility before God when you stand against the enemy, because humility breaks pride. I think James 4:7 bears repeating: "Therefore submit to God. Resist the devil and he will flee from you" (NKJV).

Also note that Jude 8–10 gives us this warning: "In the very same way, on the strength of their dreams these ungodly people pollute their own bodies, reject authority and heap abuse on celestial beings. But even the archangel Michael, when he was disputing with the devil about the body of Moses, did not himself dare to condemn him for slander but said, 'The Lord rebuke you!' Yet these people slander whatever they do not understand, and the very things they do understand by instinct—as irrational animals do—will destroy them."

Please pray:

> *Dear Lord,*
> *I also repent of any prideful words, including assumptions, curses, challenges, slander, and disrespect, I may have made (without your blessing) against any spiritual authority*

or principality I may have engaged accidentally or otherwise. I recognize that in some cases I may have stepped outside my God-given authority due to a lack of understanding. Therefore, with and through your peace, humility, and power and in the name of Jesus, I cancel any resulting assignment, scheme, or retaliation against me and my loved ones the enemy has or might evoke.

I further cancel any scheme or retaliation, discouragement, or distraction of the enemy aimed at myself or loved ones—designed to keep me from my God-given purposes and ministries.

*Because greater is he that is in me than he that is in the world (1 John 4:4), I call upon the power and authority of the name and blood of Jesus to eject, cancel, and nullify all weapons or retaliation formed against me and [name the person], including all evil plans, assignments, or works sent against me or my family (2 Cor. 10:4). As Isaiah 54:17 proclaims, "'No weapon formed against you shall prosper, and every tongue which rises against you in judgment you shall condemn. This is the heritage of the servants of the L*ORD*, and their righteousness is from Me,' says the L*ORD*" (NKJV).*

In Jesus's name, amen.

The Set Free Prayer Part 4

The next part of the set free prayer starts with a series of declarations about who you are in Christ. It also asks God to bless you with the fruit of the Spirit and ends with praise.

Dear Lord,

I declare I am forgiven of all my sins because I plead the blood of Jesus over them and because your Word says so. I also declare, through the work and authority of Jesus and the power of his blood, that I and my family are set free.

I ask you, the Lord of the universe, to replace all my sins, curses, and occultic ties and attacks with your direction and guidance, favor, grace, healing, joy, love, peace, presence, resurrection, anointing, salvation, and life.

I further declare I am who you say I am, the righteousness of Jesus Christ. Your grace is sufficient for me, and your power is made perfect in my weakness. Therefore, I can do all you say I can do. My focus is on Jesus, not the enemy. Through the power of the blood of Jesus, the enemy can't control me. Through the power of the Holy Spirit, your presence is with and in me. I am free from sin and death and alive to you in Jesus Christ. I love who I am because I am hidden in Christ (Col. 3:3). I am the righteousness of God (2 Cor. 5:21) through Jesus, and Jesus shines through me and I hear his voice. You are transforming me to be more like Jesus. To you be praise forever and ever.

Amen.

This has been an amazing time of breakthrough. Continue to pray these prayers as God lays it on your heart to do so.

As I've personally prayed these prayers these last few months, I've had breakthroughs I've sought for years. As I've given these prayers to others, they have also reported breakthroughs. A caregiver was set free from anger that was making her care for a family member almost impossible; a woman facing a shattering divorce shed her deep depression and found confidence and God's direction; a minister who had been entangled with false accusations saw the accusations disappear overnight; another man in ministry said his thinking was clearer and he found God's direction more apparent; a Christian writer had a fantastic breakthrough on placing a movie script; a woman's neck surgery was a total success; a college student passed a difficult semester; a man suffering with Alzheimer's became less confused and angry; and a man in prison, falsely accused of a crime he did not commit, is finally looking forward to parole after years of roadblocks.

But the real question is this: How will God use these prayers in your life or in the lives of your loved ones?

$\mathcal{M}$iraculous Prayer

> *Dear Lord,*
>
> *Thank you that I do not have to be fearful of the enemy. Thank you that you've given me authority and power over the enemy through the precious name and blood of your Son, Jesus.*
>
> *My eyes are on you, not the enemy. I rejoice because I get to spend eternity in heaven with you.*
>
> *In Jesus's name, amen.*

$\mathcal{S}$cripture to Ponder

(Read aloud.)

I urge you, therefore, to reaffirm your love for him. Another reason I wrote you was to see if you would stand the test and be obedient in everything. Anyone you forgive, I also forgive. And what I have forgiven—if there was anything to forgive—I have forgiven in the sight of Christ for your sake, in order that Satan might not outwit us. For we are not unaware of his schemes.

2 Corinthians 2:8–11

To see Linda's interview about the story of Satan, go to www. NeedMiracleBook.com or turn to page 206 for a QR code.

8

More Strategies
for Fighting the Enemy

Resist the devil, and he will flee from you.

James 4:7 KJV

Convinced spiritual warfare is silly? Then imagine strolling through a slithering viper pit, blindfolded. I mean, just because you can't see the enemy doesn't mean he's not there and poised to strike. Perhaps with this idea in mind, we should take 1 Peter 5:8–9 to heart: "Stay alert! Watch out for your great enemy, the devil. He prowls around like a roaring lion, looking for someone to devour. Stand firm against him, and be strong in your faith" (NLT).

So as Peter says, "Stay alert!" Take your blindfold off and discover some strategies to help you avoid the enemy's pits and attacks all together. And if you find yourself in trouble, these strategies may contain the secret to help you break free.

Strategies to Fight the Enemy

In his book *When the Enemy Strikes*, Charles Stanley explains why Satan comes against us.

> He can and will attempt to drag you down into such deep bondage that you will lose your joy in living. Some may call this bondage oppression, depression, or addiction. If the devil can pull you into bondage, you will have no peace, no zest for living, and perhaps even no will to continue living. You will struggle continually with desires that are not met, drives that are not satisfied, dreams that are not realized, and a destiny that is not fulfilled. The devil will do his utmost to destroy anything that is essential for abundant life.[1]

Sometimes we hear God's still, small voice in our inner ear, and sometimes we hear the enemy tempting us into discouragement, sin, or even death.

But what this really means is that when we realize we have authority over the enemy, we can live a life filled with miracles as we learn how to keep our joy; avoid pitfalls; retain our zest and will for living; see our desires, dreams, and destiny fulfilled; and experience God's abundant life.

So in addition to praying the set free prayer from the previous chapter, you may want to try these additional warfare strategies as you discover even more avenues to miracles as these prayers will help you:

- stop the voices
- stop the spirit of suicide and discouragement
- break the bondage of the generations
- break your own curses

- bless your home
- break false judgments and rejection
- break unhealthy connections

Stop the Voices

Not every thought that passes through your mind originates with you. Sometimes we hear God's still, small voice in our inner ear, and sometimes we hear the enemy tempting us into discouragement, sin, or even death.

I recently got a phone call from a Chicago policeman who, though he loved his family, was overwhelmed by financial pressures. Through his tears he said, "I keep thinking God is telling me if I walk away from my family, the financial pressures will stop and everything will be okay."

I said, "Do you love your family?"

The man wept harder. "Very much."

"Do you want to leave them?"

"I really don't."

"Then what makes you think the message to leave your family is coming from God?"

"What do you mean?"

"Well, I already know it's not God's will that you leave your family. So what you're hearing is a message from the enemy."

He was shocked. "You mean like Satan?"

"Yes. He's sent a demon to taunt you with this message—a message meant to discourage and deceive you. Satan wants to destroy you and your family."

"What can I do?"

"Tell this demon to be silent in the name of Jesus. Tell it that its assignment is canceled through the authority and power of the name and blood of Jesus."

"I can do that?"

"You certainly can."

This dear man was relieved to discover that he did not have to follow this insistent voice and that he could trust in and claim God's power to stop it.

Friends, it's time to get mad about these messages the enemy is sending us, our family, and friends, and it's time to tell the enemy to be quiet. And yes, when we call on the name of Jesus, we have the power to do just that, which is in itself a miracle.

Stop the Spirit of Suicide and Discouragement

My friend Joy and I visited with a woman who told us her husband, Toby, had spent an evening with their depressed son. By the time Toby left at midnight, their son Logan felt better and said, "Don't worry, Dad, I'm going to be okay. I promise I won't do anything foolish."

But an hour later, Logan went down to his garage, shut the door, and turned on his car's engine. His roommate found him a few hours later, barely alive.

When Logan had recovered well enough to talk to his family, he told them he'd been fine when his dad had left, but then at one in the morning, an inner voice began to mock him, saying, *You have no hope. You have nothing to live for.*

When his mother, Carla, finished telling the story, Joy told her, "Your son heard a parroting spirit."

"What's that?" Carla asked.

Joy explained, "A parroting spirit is when a lower-class demon is sent on an assignment to parrot or continually repeat a distressing message to a person. A phrase like, 'I can't take anymore, I can't take anymore,' seeks to open the door to suicidal suggestion." Joy said, "The solution is to tell this demon to be quiet in the name of Jesus. Next, tell it you are canceling its assignment to harass your son by the authority of the name of Jesus and through the power of his blood."

If you're wondering what demonic messages aimed at you might sound like, I can tell you they are filled with discouraging ideas, such as, "You are stupid, fat, or ugly." "No one can love you." "No one even likes you." "There is no hope." "You will fail."

If you have thoughts like these, it's time to go to war. Tell the voice to be silent and that its assignment is canceled in the power and authority of the name and blood of Jesus.

Next, pick up your Bible and read the Word, perhaps Ephesians 3:17–19: "May your roots go down deep into the soil of God's marvelous love; and may you be able to feel and under-

> *Know the enemy is terrified of the "real" you, a person who knows who you are in Christ Jesus and exercises the authority Christ has given you.*

stand, as all God's children should, how long, how wide, how deep, and how high his love really is; and to experience this love for yourselves, though it is so great that you will never see the end of it or fully know or understand it. And so at last you will be filled up with God himself" (TLB).

If the harassment continues, quote Scripture to the demon. For example, you could say, "The Word says, 'God's love for me is wide, deep, and high and so big I will never see the end of it,' so be silent in the power and authority of the name and blood of Jesus. You have no right to discourage me, for I am a child of the King."

In case you're wondering, messages from God's Holy Spirit sound like, "I love you, my child. I am with you. Everything is going to be okay. Trust me."

There's no comparison between God's voice and the enemy's voice—one conveys hateful discouragement and the other loving encouragement. So as soon as you recognize the source of your discouraging thoughts, fight back. Know the enemy is terrified of the "real" you, a person who knows who you are in Christ Jesus and exercises the authority Christ has given you.

Also, if you find you are being constantly reminded of an offense you've already forgiven, a parroting demon may be behind this assault. But don't get frustrated. Instead, remind the enemy the offense in question has already been forgiven through the power of Jesus and is under the blood of Jesus. Next, tell the demon to be quiet in the name and power of Jesus.

You may have to repeat the warfare prayer a few more times, but the enemy will retreat when he catches on that you're no longer open to reviving old grudges.

Break the Bondage of the Generations

Have you ever stopped to think that the enemy has done plenty of research on you? I mean, he knows everyone in your family line all the way back to Adam. He also remembers which schemes worked best on those ancestors who were most like you. In fact, he's tripped generations of the "dear and departed" with tried-and-true issues and sins. And he uses his collected data against you and your children. *How's that for unfair?*

Well, no worries. Even if you have problems similar to those in past generations, including a pet sin that's been hidden in the family, a tie to the occult, a curse, or even a blood oath spoken by someone in your family tree, you can pray against it with a prayer as simple as:

> *Dear Lord,*
> *I plead Jesus's blood over myself, my children, and my family.*
> *Please break any curse or familiar sin such as _____,*
> *or blood oath such as _____, or occultic tie*

such as _____ connected to myself, my family,
and my children in the power of the name and blood of Jesus.
   In Jesus's name, amen.

(Fill in the blanks, if you know what the blanks are. Otherwise, just pray this prayer without including the "such as" portions.)

Can a prayer like this lead to a miracle? Ask Sean. His father was an alcoholic, so it was no small wonder that Sean became a drug addict at the age of thirteen. His mother and sisters had no idea that he was involved in drugs, even though he had three hospitalized overdoses as an adult. They thought his seizures were epileptic, but when they learned the truth, they committed to praying against this curse of the generations. It took years, but when Sean was forty-six, he turned back to the Lord and was immediately freed from his addiction and has remained free—thanks to God answering the warfare prayers of his mother and sisters.

Break Your Own Curses

If you are the one who is cursing yourself or others, it's time to watch your mouth. James said about the tongue, "It is always ready to pour out its deadly poison. Sometimes it praises our heavenly Father, and sometimes it breaks out into curses against men who are made like God. And so blessing and cursing come pouring out of the same mouth. Dear brothers, surely this is not right!" (James 3:8–10 TLB).

Here's an example of what I am talking about. Phoebe was often exasperated by the antics of her children, so she'd scold them with, "You'll all wind up in jail."

Twenty years later, after each of Phoebe's adult children had been sentenced to jail terms, she realized the power of her words against her kids. She asked me, "Do you think my words gave the enemy legal authority over my kids in this area?"

I told her, "I'd have to say it's a strong possibility, especially when you consider Scripture passages such as, 'Death and life are in the power of the tongue' (Prov. 18:21 NKJV)."

Phoebe sought God's forgiveness for her careless words and prayed to break their curse. She's since begun to see break-throughs for her children. Phoebe now uses her words to bless and encourage her children as she continues to pray for them.

Be careful with your words and wrestle back any spiritual authority you may have inadvertently given the enemy with careless talk. This includes the phrase, "I wish I were dead."

My friend Joy believes that verbally expressing that wish is like agreeing with the enemy to put a spirit of death in your life—to come against your God-given dreams, relationships, and destiny. So if you've been guilty of verbalizing this death wish or thoughts of suicide, pray:

> *Dear Lord,*
> *I renounce my death wish and/or spirit of suicide and choose life, your abundant life. Forgive me for my careless words. I break any spirit of suicide and cancel any curse or assignment of the enemy my words may have generated in the power and authority of the name and blood of Jesus.*
> *In Jesus's name, amen.*

At one of my recent prayer conferences, Skyler pulled me aside. "I'm glad you talked about this because I've often 'wished I was dead,' and when I prayed along with you, I felt like I was given a new beginning." Skyler emailed me a few weeks later to confirm her breakthrough had been genuine. "I just wanted you to know that I am now free of suicidal thoughts and I have a fresh excitement in my walk with Christ. Thanks for teaching me how to pray against a curse I'd accidently put on myself. Being free of it has been like a miracle."

Bless Your Home

Have you ever walked through your house or dwelling and asked God to bless each room with the power of the blood of Jesus? It's a nice thing to do, but let me caution you. The first time I ever blessed my home, my beautiful and healthy dog, a snow-white Samoyed, walked into the one room I had *not* prayed over and fell over dead. I don't know exactly why this happened, but nevertheless, I count it as a warning. If you decide to bless your home (and you should), please remember to pray over every room, bathroom, and hallway, including the garage, porch, closets, attic, breezeway, and basement.

Also, some people like to mark the doorposts and window tops of each room with a finger-drawn cross made from olive oil as they pray. It serves as a reminder of the original Passover in Egypt when the Israelites marked their doorposts with the blood of a lamb. To bless your home, please pray:

> *Dear Lord,*
> *Bless my home with your presence through the power of the blood of Jesus. In the authority and power of the name and blood of Jesus, I command any unclean spirit to leave every room, attic, staircase, closet, garage, hallway, driveway, yard, porch, crawl space, and any other area in my house. Lord, I ask you to send your angels to guard every entrance. Please protect my home from the enemy or any other disaster.*
> *In Jesus's name, amen.*

Since I've finished praying over my home, I can tell you that God's peace has rested there. If you need the miracle of peace in your home, do not hesitate to pray through your house. And no worries, if you pray the prayer above, there will be no over-looked areas for the enemy to lurk.

Break False Judgments and Rejection

A few months ago, I faced a difficult truth: many people whom I considered important to me had simply vanished from my life. Years before, one dear friend had falsely accused me of saying something I hadn't said. She was hurt and told me we could no longer be friends. My apologies and protests did nothing to help the situation, and she parted ways with me.

A few years later, a colleague started a false rumor about me, one she apparently believed.

Then one of my best friends moved away when her husband took a job out of state. That wasn't as hard as when she suddenly ignored my attempts to reach out to her. It was as if I had offended her, but how?

As I thought about these losses, my heart grieved. But it dawned on me that I was looking at the work of the enemy. When I realized he had come against my most cherished relationships with lies, deceit, rejection, and false judgments, I instantly went to prayer:

> *Dear Lord,*
>
> *I forgive those who have judged me unfairly, gossiped about me, rejected me, or believed a lie about me. I realize the enemy is the author of false judgments, rejection, and lies. Therefore, I break the assignments and consequences of false judgments, rejection, and lies connected to me in the power and authority of the name and blood of Jesus. I ask you to restore my precious relationships. I also ask you to grant me your grace and favor in my relationships with others.*
>
> *In Jesus's name, amen.*

The next day, a miracle occurred. Although I'd told no one of my prayer, my former best friend sent me a five-page email, full of cheerful news. What made this unusual was that it was the first time she'd contacted me in fourteen years. A few days later, the one who had started the rumor about me called me and told me she knew the thing she'd believed about me was untrue. We joyfully reconciled. Then a few weeks after that, the one who had falsely believed I'd said a hurtful thing invited me over. Over coffee she told me how much she loved me and that I was one of her dearest friends. I was overjoyed to have these precious relationships restored.

But how like the enemy, that great deceiver, to put false judgments, rejection, and stumbling blocks of deceit into some of my dearest relationships.

But how like the enemy, that great deceiver, to put false judgments, rejection, and stumbling blocks of deceit into some of my dearest relationships. If you think this may have happened to you, your friends, and loved ones, first pray the prayer from above, then add:

> *Dear Lord,*
>
> *If I've believed a lie, rejected, or been deceived about a friend, colleague, or family member, please forgive me. Open my eyes to the truth. Please restore our relationship.*
>
> *In Jesus's name, amen.*

As I've prayed this second prayer, I've come to realize the best about certain people I'd formally believed the worst about. I too was deceived in some of my relationships with others. How glad I am that Jesus set me free.

Did you know we can also have false judgments against God, especially when we believe our difficulties and disasters serve as evidence that he doesn't love us? If you think you could be guilty of believing this lie, please pray:

> Dear Lord,
> If the enemy has deceived me regarding your love for me or any other lies concerning you, please forgive me. Please open my eyes so I can see I am your adored child. Help me to see other truths about you that I've misunderstood. I break the enemy's deception from our relationship in the power and authority of the name and blood of Jesus. For your truth will set me free.
> In Jesus's name, amen.

There's one more person we often have false judgment against: ourselves. Remember the Chicago policeman I told you about? As we chatted by phone, he confessed he and his wife had almost aborted their son. They'd actually made an appointment, kept it, but chickened out in the waiting room. This dear man was convinced their "almost" deed had not only cursed their young son but would also cause something terrible to happen to their family. He said, "When I read your book *When You Don't Know How to Pray* and saw how you had almost killed (euthanized) your daughter when she was in a coma, I realized you were the same as me. I thought, if she's not cursed because of what she almost did, then maybe there's hope for me."

Do you see the lie the enemy used to deceive this dear father? It was, "Because you *almost* did a terrible thing, you and your family are cursed."

I told this dad the truth. "The enemy knows, even before birth, whom God has anointed. He often tempts the parents of these special children to terminate their lives.

"Don't you see? Your family and son are not cursed because of this incident. God intervened, and you and your wife escaped the abortion clinic with your son, alive! God saved your son for a special purpose. You, your son, and family are blessed."

As for those who have lost children to abortion, let me throw my arms around you and tell you how much the Lord loves you. However, you do need to humbly go to God regarding this issue. Repent and determine not to abort another child for the sake of convenience, timing, or lack of trust in God. Ask the Lord to break the curse from yourself and your descendants. Then rejoice that your child is with God and will someday meet you in heaven. With all forgiven, you are free to grow in your love relationship with the Lord.

Break Unhealthy Connections

Unhealthy connections occur when one person's soul is bound to another person's soul through the act of sex outside of marriage. Genesis 2:24 says, "That is why a man leaves his father and mother and is united to his wife, and they become one flesh."

C. S. Lewis's *Screwtape Letters* portrays a senior demon training an inexperienced demon. The senior demon explains God's design for human sexuality by saying, "Now comes the joke. The Enemy [God] described a married couple as 'one flesh.' He did not say 'a happily married couple' or a 'couple who married because they were in love,' but you can make humans ignore that. You can also make them forget the man they call Paul did not confine it to married couples. Mere copulation, for him, makes 'one flesh' (Eph. 5:31)."[2]

Later, the senior demon explains, "The truth is that whenever a man lies with a woman, there, whether they like it or not, a transcendental relationship is set up between them that must be eternally enjoyed or eternally endured."[3]

So in other words, a person is somehow still tied in a deep, soul-level union with every person with whom they've slept. However, these soul-ties may not have to be "eternally endured" if God himself sets you free. For example, Lisa's husband left her for another woman. Lisa confided, "Though ten years have passed, it's as if the pain is as fresh as the day he told me he was leaving."

Lisa had an unbroken "soul-tie," meaning her soul was still tied with her ex-husband's through the act of marriage. I led her to pray a simple prayer. "Dear Lord, please break the soul-tie Lisa shares with her ex. In Jesus's name, amen."[4]

A year later, Lisa told me, "Since I prayed with you, I've been totally free of the emotional tie I had with Clint. It's like I'm a new person: a person who's been freed of a heartbreaking bond."[5]

If you are soul-bound to others from your past, please pray:

> Dear Lord,
> I confess and repent of any sin regarding my past sexual relationship with [name all or ask God to bring them to mind]. Please forgive me, Lord. I bring this/these unwanted soul-tie(s) to you. Please break this/these soul-tie(s) through the power and authority of the name and blood of Jesus.
> In Jesus's name, amen.

If you have a soul-tie with someone because you were the victim of rape, sexual abuse, or incest, please pray:

> Dear Lord,
> I bring to you this great wrong that was done to me, and I choose to forgive, not through my power but through your power, because it's time I was set free. Please break this soul-tie to _____ through the power and authority of the name and blood of Jesus.
> In Jesus's name, amen.

Rejoice! You are free indeed.

ℳiraculous Prayer

Dear Lord,

I am so glad your Son died for my sins. I am so glad that when I make a mistake I can come to you, repent, and receive full forgiveness. What a miracle your forgiveness is. Thank you that this is the start of an even bigger miracle you are doing in my life. Thank you for these breakthrough prayers and the resulting miracles that will transform my life and the lives of my loved ones.

I praise and worship you.

In Jesus's name, amen.

Scripture to Ponder

(Read aloud.)

This is all the more urgent, for you know how late it is; time is running out. Wake up, for our salvation is nearer now than when we first believed. The night is almost gone; the day of salvation will soon be here. So remove your dark deeds like dirty clothes, and put on the shining armor of right living. Because we belong to the day, we must live decent lives for all to see. Don't participate in the darkness of wild parties and drunkenness, or in sexual promiscuity and immoral living, or in quarreling and jealousy.

Romans 13:11–13 NLT

For more warfare strategies, watch Linda interview Becky Harling at www.NeedMiracleBook.com or turn to page 206 for a QR code.

9

The Praise Factor

I will bless the LORD at all times;
His praise shall continually be in my mouth.

Psalm 34:1 NKJV

Not long ago, I was in a wonderful worship service. The lights were low and the level of worship was high. As I closed my eyes and praised God, I found myself in a place of golden lamp stands topped with smoking clay lamps. I saw Jesus walking among the lamp stands. He was garbed in a white robe with a golden sash that crossed his chest from one shoulder to his waist. His hair was white as wool and his skin glowed bronze. His brown eyes were like blazing fire. I quietly watched him as the praise of the worshipers became whiffs of smoke rising from the clay lamps. I saw Jesus breathe in the smoke, and as he exhaled, I saw his very breath fill the lungs of the worshipers, making the breath of Jesus the very air they breathed. As

I marveled at this, Jesus turned to me, his eyes gentle but fiery. "I see you," he said.

I was so shocked that he acknowledged me. I opened my eyes and saw I was still standing in the worship service.

Though I can't explain the why or the how of this experience, it reminds me of Psalm 22:3, which says, "But thou art holy, O thou that inhabitest the praises of Israel" (KJV).

Does God really inhabit our praise?

Let's take a closer look. The word for "inhabitest" is actually the Hebrew word *yashab*, pronounced (yaw-shab'); its meanings include to abide, continue, dwell, endure, establish, and inhabit.[1]

If we want more of God, his miracles and presence, we need to spend more time worshiping him. But praising God accomplishes a lot more than meets the eye. For example, praise can help establish the miracles that will:

- help us become a living sacrifice
- help us hear God's voice
- help us win the battle
- lead us to the miraculous breakthrough

Helps Us Become a Living Sacrifice

Because Jesus sacrificed himself for us, we no longer have to offer the blood of bulls and goats on the altar as a payment for our sin. However, we can offer ourselves as a *living* sacrifice to God as an act of love (Rom. 12:1). One of the best ways to do so is to give our time and devotion to God as gifts of praise. In fact, many biblical greats offered God the sacrifice of praise just before God turned their dire circumstances into a miracle, like the time God set the captives free and restored the lost land of Israel (Jer. 33:11).

Jonah, despite his circumstances, offered the Lord the sacrifice of praise from the belly of the whale: "But I, with shouts of grateful praise, will sacrifice to you" (Jonah 2:9). Then moments later, the whale spat Jonah onto dry land so Jonah could continue his journey to Nineveh. There, the people turned back to God and were spared God's wrath.

The sacrifice of praise was also included in the 107th psalm, a psalm of worship thought to have been used to rededicate the temple following the Israelites' return from captivity. "Let them sacrifice the sacrifices of thanksgiving, and declare His works with rejoicing" (v. 22 NKJV).

The sacrifice of praise is still an important part of our relationship with God. Paul said in Hebrews 13:15, "Therefore by Him let us continually offer the sacrifice of praise to God, that is, the fruit of our lips, giving thanks to His name" (NKJV).

What would such a sacrifice of praise look like? My friend Rose recently demonstrated it when she came to me in tears. It seems her family is hopelessly in debt, just at a time when they should be enjoying their retirement years. She told me, "But we know we're going to be okay."

"How do you know?" I asked.

"Because we're praising God. You see, we have been believing, following, and trusting God for thirty years. We know from experience that God will see us through, so we continue to trust and praise him."

Now, that's beautiful. I know God will be their provider because whenever I've found myself in lack, I've applied this same principle of praise, and watched as God provided for my needs, like the time my daughter's hospital bill totaled over a million dollars following her four months of hospitalization after our car accident. I decided not to panic, but praised God for his provision. The result? The bill was unexpectedly paid in full through a brand-new insurance policy that was still being processed at the time of the accident.

The reason God wants us to praise him is not because he needs to be reminded he is great; it's because we need to be reminded that the presence of a great God abides with us. When we worship him, we focus on him, and that focus builds trust. God often responds to our worship by answering our prayers and setting the captives free.

Take a moment to offer your own sacrifice of praise:

> *Dear Lord,*
>
> *I come to you with a sacrifice of praise. I know you are great and majestic, far above any problem I face. I give thanks to you, for you are good and your mercy endures forever. I worship you and you alone. I praise your holy name. Thank you that you'll answer my prayers with miracles and set the captives free.*
>
> *In Jesus's name, amen.*

Helps Us Hear God's Voice

When Stormie Omartian's husband wanted to move from California to Tennessee, Stormie wasn't so sure it was God's ideal for them. But Stormie's husband, Michael, was wise enough to turn over the job of convincing her to God.

As Stormie began her journey to seek God's will, whenever she'd become fearful, she'd praise God for his perfect will, revelation, and wisdom. During one such praise session, she got a clear impression that, yes, she and her husband were to move to Tennessee. She knew it was God because it was not a conclusion she'd have made on her own.

Stormie said, "And we certainly needed that solid knowledge of God's will because of the three years of storms (literally) and trials and monumental challenges that were to come once we moved. Had we not known for certain that the move was God's will, we might have entertained the idea of moving back. We would have thought we had made a mistake. And amazingly enough, I was the one who had to convince my husband a few times that we were right where God wanted us."[2]

Stormie reminds us, "When we praise our all-wise, all-knowing God, the very act of praising Him opens the channel through which He imparts His wisdom and a knowledge of His will to us. That is the hidden power of praising God."[3]

> *"When we praise our all-wise, all-knowing God, the very act of praising Him opens the channel through which He imparts His wisdom and a knowledge of His will to us."*

When my friend Joy was first learning how to praise God in everything, she was experiencing a problem with her lawn. No matter how much she watered it, spent money on fertilizers and treatments, the lawn continued to die. So she prayed, "Lord, though I don't understand why I have a brown lawn or what's going on with it, I praise you anyway."

Shortly thereafter, she called someone to see about a problem with her sprinkler. But when the repairman began to dig, he said, "Lady, you've got a problem with sod webworms."

As soon as Joy understood the problem, it was a quick and simple solution to green her lawn. Joy says, "It was a great way to see how God responded to my praise. He soon provided me with the wisdom I needed to resolve my problem."

Let's praise God so he will miraculously reveal his will and wisdom to us:

> *Dear Lord,*
> *As I seek your will in the area(s) of _____,*
> *I trust and praise you for your perfect will, revelation, and wisdom. Thank you for never being too late to show and teach*

me what I need to know. Thank you for guiding me. I worship,
praise, and adore you, for you are great. You are my provider,
my salvation, and my Lord.
    In Jesus's name, amen.

Helps Us Win the Battle

Praise helps us to rehearse all the reasons God is great. It reminds us we're worshiping the one who can provide for and dwell in our every circumstance. In fact, when we compare focusing on God through worship to focusing on the difficulties of our problems, we can see there's no comparison. Focusing on God gives us hope. Focusing on our difficulties is like placing our difficulties above our hope in God.

When we focus on God by praising him, we're not denying our problems exist; we're denying that the power of our problems is greater than the power of God. Is there a problem God can't solve? Is his arm ever too short? Is there a difficulty he can't turn into good? Is there any miracle he can't perform?

As you begin to understand that God is in fact the solution to all your problems, you'll be more inspired to praise him. As you do, he will abide with and inhabit you.

Consider David's response to the problem of Goliath, the nine-foot-tall champion of the armies of the Philistines (1 Sam. 17). When David, the little brother of a couple of the Israelite soldiers, showed up at camp to bring his brothers cheese and bread, David heard Goliath's taunts: "Choose a man for yourselves, and let him come down to me. If he is able to fight with me and kill me, then we will be your servants. But if I prevail against him and kill him, then you shall be our servants and serve us" (vv. 8–9 NKJV).

David was surprised no man was willing to confront Goliath and said so to his brothers. His words were repeated to King Saul, and Saul called for this shepherd boy to stand before him.

There David argued that *he* be allowed to face Goliath, saying, "The LORD, who delivered me from the paw of the lion and from the paw of the bear, He will deliver me from the hand of this Philistine" (v. 37 NKJV).

Saul allowed the match and ordered David to wear the king's own armor, but David cast it aside, complaining he wasn't used to it. So David went to meet Goliath with only his shepherd's staff, his slingshot, and five smooth stones from the nearby brook. When Goliath saw the lad holding a staff and a slingshot, he couldn't believe his eyes. "Am I a dog, that you come to me with sticks?" (v. 43 NKJV).

David retorted, "You come to me with a sword, with a spear, and with a javelin. But I come to you in the name of the LORD of hosts, the God of the armies of Israel, whom you have defied. This day the LORD will deliver you into my hand, and I will strike you and take your head from you. And this day I will give the carcasses of the camp of the Philistines to the birds of the air and the wild beasts of the earth, that all the earth may know that there is a God in Israel. Then all this assembly shall know that the LORD does not save with sword and spear; for the battle is the LORD's, and He will give you into our hands" (vv. 45–47 NKJV).

> *Through praise, we can be like David and can trust God with our problem, proving that our God is bigger than anything we might face.*

Then David ran toward Goliath, reached his hand into his pocket, grabbed a stone, fitted it into his slingshot, and *zing*. In an instant, the stone struck the forehead of the giant. Goliath was dead before his body hit the ground.

Through praise, we can be like David and can trust God with our problem, proving that our God is bigger than anything we might face.

David Jeremiah said, "When we go forth into the battle—whether we battle through a family crisis or a career problem—we have two strategies. We can go in our own weakness and face defeat, or we can take the power of the Lord with us. How do we do the latter? We simply love, adore, worship, and praise His name. We know God makes His home in our praises, and He will march with us even unto the farthest corners of the earth and the end of the age. As we worship, our life strategies come together in ways we could never have formulated on our own."[4]

Let's follow David's example and pray:

> *Dear Lord,*
>
> *Despite the problems before me, I put my hope in you, Lord. For who or what are these problems compared to you? You are the mighty God of the universe who also loves and cares for me. Therefore, I also put my trust in you. I believe you can conquer any circumstances and troubles I face and turn them into miracles. I know you will deliver me from my enemies and troubles.*
>
> *Thank you, Lord. I praise and trust in you. Who is like you? In Jesus's name, amen.*

Leads Us to the Miraculous Breakthrough

Have you noticed that sometimes everything seems lost just before a breakthrough? Think about Paul and Silas. They were in the worst of circumstances, having been beaten and tossed into prison for the crime of sharing their faith. But despite it all—the bruises, the indignity, the jailhouse conditions—they were praising God, as we read in Acts 16: "Around midnight Paul and Silas were praying and singing hymns to God, and the other prisoners were listening. Suddenly, there was a massive earthquake, and the prison was shaken to its foundations. All the doors immediately flew open, and the chains of every prisoner fell off!" (vv. 25–26 NLT).

Their praises, combined with the power of God, broke their chains, as well as the chains of all who were with them. Why? For one thing, praising God when things aren't going our way is another example of the sacrifice of praise—a sacrifice God loves to honor. In fact, moments after the earthquake, Paul and Silas were privileged to lead the jailer and his entire family out of their spiritual chains to faith in Jesus. The irony is that such an act of evangelism may well have been what got Paul and Silas arrested in the first place.

> *Their praises, combined with the power of God, broke their chains, as well as the chains of all who were with them.*

To illustrate this point of sacrificial praise even further, let me tell you about a day my friend Ashly had everything go wrong, the very day she'd sought God for a miracle. Ashly said, "But I decided I could trust God anyway. It was hard, but I spent the day praising him because, after all, he knows what he's doing."

The following day, Ashly had unbelievable breakthroughs. Not only did the things that had gone wrong straighten out, but they also turned into miracles. Ashly later said, "It was as if the miracles were God's way of telling me he took pleasure in my obedience when I praised him though everything went wrong."

I can't promise that praising God will always result in the miracle you are hoping for, but do it anyway, because it's the will of God. First Thessalonians 5:17–18 says, "Pray continually, give thanks in all circumstances; for this is God's will for you in Christ Jesus."

When my friend Carole was diagnosed with a hefty tumor on her pancreas, instead of panicking, she spent time praising God.

She continually prayed, "My cyst has no right to exist, thank you Lord for healing me," for several weeks. Then, when she went in for surgery, the doctor decided to take one more picture only to discover her tumor had disappeared. Carole said, "Do you know what a miracle that is? I once read in *Forbes* magazine that only four hundred people have actual documentation that their tumors went into remission without treatment."

Without treatment? Well, Carole treated her tumor with praise unto God, and as a result, God showed he was bigger than her tumor when it ceased to exist.

Now, as promised, I will tell you the rest of my brother's story. As you might recall, I left you with the doctor telling my parents my brother's chances of survival were slim.

Despite the fact that the doctors didn't expect Jimmy to live through the day, he did. "Still," the doctors told my parents, "your son is in a coma, and he probably will never wake up. If he does, he'll most likely be brain damaged."

However, Jimmy woke up the next day and began to scribble, "What happened to me?" "Was anyone else hurt?" and finally, "I love you." Still, the doctors seemed unimpressed. "Certainly," they said, "Jimmy will never walk again. He crushed his fifth and sixth thoracic vertebrae and suffered kidney and liver damage; no one ever recovers from that."

But what these doctors hadn't counted on was the power of a grateful heart combined with the power of God. Jimmy continued to heal. Why? I believe it was because, as my nineteen-year-old brother lay in his hospital bed, he called out to God, not to scold, "God, how dare you allow this to happen to me?" but to whisper, "Thank you, Lord, thank you," each time he had the slightest improvement.

For example, when he was able to move his big toe for the first time, he did not pray, "Lord, give me more, more, more. . ."

Instead, he prayed, "Lord, thank you so much that I can move my toe. I'm so grateful to you."

He'd repeat his prayers of gratitude as God continued to heal him on each new level. "Lord, thank you that I can bend my knee." "Thank you that I can stand." "Lord, thank you that I can lift my foot."

Then came the day Jimmy walked his lovely bride, Mary, back down the aisle after they said their "I do's." Now, two children later, we can say the doctors were certainly wrong. God healed my brother.

With God, healings of any kind are possible.

Okay, I know I said there is no formula for miracles, but let me contradict myself. The formula for miracles is this: an all-powerful God + a grateful, believing heart + God's will = a miracle.

I agree with Beth Moore when she said, "Please understand. Christ is fully God. He can heal anyone or perform any wonder, whether the belief of the person is great or small. Christ isn't asking us to believe in our ability to exercise unwavering faith, He is asking us to believe He is able."[5]

Beth continues, "When it comes to bringing us to a life of freedom, I believe He is also willing. If we're focusing on physical healing, I would not have such certainty. Sometimes God heals physical sicknesses, and sometimes He chooses greater glory through illnesses. He can always heal physical diseases, but He does not always choose to bring healing on this earth."

The formula for miracles is this: an all-powerful God + a grateful, believing heart + God's will = a miracle.

I believe Beth got it right. But she also talks of a circumstance God always wants to heal when she said, "Scripture is absolutely clear, however, that God always wills the spiritual captive to be free."[6]

Let's apply what we learned about miraculous prayer by praying.

*M*iraculous Prayer

Dear Lord,

I know you see me. I want to express my love and gratitude to you, for even in my difficulties, you are there, working it all out for the good. I praise you in the difficulties, and I also praise you for my blessings, as well as my answers to prayer. I thank you because I know you know what you are doing and I trust you.

I also ask, if it be your will, that you'd grant my request of _____. Thank you that I can ask you. Thank you that you hear. Thank you that you are able to do even more than I ask for. I believe you are able. Thank you that regardless of how you answer, you will be with me and you will turn this situation into a miracle. I trust you, dear Lord.

In Jesus's name, amen.

*S*cripture to Ponder

(Read aloud)

> I waited patiently for the LORD;
>   he turned to me and heard my cry.
> He lifted me out of the slimy pit,
>   out of the mud and mire;
> he set my feet on a rock
>   and gave me a firm place to stand.
> He put a new song in my mouth,
>   a hymn of praise to our God.

Many will see and fear the LORD
and put their trust in him.

Psalm 40:1–3

Watch Linda's praise interview at www.NeedMiracleBook.
com or turn to page 206 for a QR code.

10

The Sold Out Factor

But seek first his kingdom and his righteousness, and all these things will be given to you as well.

Matthew 6:33

What would happen if everyone who reads this book dedicated a year to living sold out for God? If even twenty thousand readers pledged to do so, the world would receive the gift of twenty thousand years of service to God in one year. Can you imagine how that kind of power would change the world?

What would happen if *you* lived sold out for God? Well, if you really want to see miracles in your life, perhaps you should make this very commitment and pray:

> *Dear Lord,*
> *I ask you to make your desires my desires. I commit to following wherever you lead, sold out to you. I can't wait to see the resulting miracles.*
> *In Jesus's name, amen.*

151

Let me tell you about a band of men who live this pledge in an inner-city Denver neighborhood.

My producer told me, "Linda, as you get to know these guys from Set Free Church, you're going to find out they're modern-day disciples."

When I first met them in the green room of a Denver television studio, I discovered they were a scruffy group, looking as though they still rode with their former motorcycle gangs.

Later, as we sat in front of the cameras, the men told a little about their church and how the power of Jesus had set each of them free from addictions as well as their former gang lifestyle. However, their most passionate message came when Frenchy, with tears in his eyes, said, "We're determined to give a toy to every child in the inner city of Denver who needs one. In fact, if anyone watching has a child who needs a toy this Christmas, call us and we will make sure your child gets a toy."

What would happen if you lived sold out for God?

As it was already December, I timidly ventured, "Have you collected a lot of toys?"

Frenchy never blinked at the eye of the camera. "No."

"Do you have money for toys?"

Frenchy lifted his chin. "No. But God will bring us the toys."

I turned to the camera. "There may be *one* person watching who has enough toys to meet this entire need."

After the studio lights winked off, I drove home a bit troubled by both Frenchy's boldness and the group's lack of resources. *Would God really provide?*

A year later, Trish, my producer, called to say, "Frenchy and the men from Set Free Church are coming back to the studio this week."

"Whatever happened to their toy drive last year?"

Trish laughed. "Didn't you hear? There was a woman watching the show that morning, and when you said how one person could supply the need for all the toys, she knew you were talking about her."

"No kidding?"

"It seems she'd been collecting toys at yard sales to sell on eBay. But when she saw the show, she decided God was calling her to give her toys to Set Free Church. It took the men more than six trips with their vans to get them all."

Later, in the studio, Frenchy reported, "We had enough toys to give five hundred inner-city kids five toys each, plus we helped fill the needs of three other toy banks."

But the generosity of Set Free Church doesn't stop at toy drives. Though the church doesn't have even one wealthy member, it seems no one has told them they're not rich enough to do all God has called them to do. In fact, every week, the church provides tons of food to struggling families by gleaning unused food from grocery stores and restaurants. They have so much food that they have enough to meet the needs of not only their community but also nine other food banks in other neighborhoods.

These believers enjoy so many miracles because they're sold out, ready and willing to follow God.

How Do We Live Sold Out?

If we want to live sold out lives, we need to:

- understand that we do not belong to ourselves
- understand that the Holy Spirit dwells in us
- ignite the Holy Spirit with the power of God's Word
- ask for wisdom

Understand That We Do Not Belong to Ourselves

You were bought at a price (1 Cor. 6:20) and therefore do not belong to yourself. In fact, Jeremiah 10:23 says, "Lord, I know that people's lives are not their own; it is not for them to direct their steps."

If you're not sure if you've totally given up your so-called control to God, now may be the time to pray:

> *Dear Lord,*
>
> *I confess I belong to you, not myself. Forgive me for living as though I'd forgotten this. Jesus paid the price for me with his precious blood, buying me from the kingdom of darkness so I can walk with him in his kingdom of light. Therefore, I want to live sold out for you. Lead me, teach me, guide me. I dedicate my life to you.*
>
> *In Jesus's name, amen.*

Understand That the Holy Spirit Dwells in Us

We know that when we're in Christ, the Holy Spirit is in us. First Corinthians 6:19 says, "Do you not know that your bodies are temples of the Holy Spirit, who is in you, whom you have received from God?"

We need to acknowledge the presence of the Holy Spirit by honoring God with our bodies and by refraining from wrong.

We also recognize the Holy Spirit is in us by praying:

> *Dear Lord,*
>
> *Forgive me if I've not been honoring the Holy Spirit's presence within me. Help me to remember that my body is his temple. Help my body-temple to be a welcome place for him not only to indwell but also to increase. May I be so filled with the Holy*

154

Spirit's presence that it shines, ignites, and spills out of my life and into the lives of others. Give me more of the Holy Spirit's presence.

In Jesus's name, amen.

Ignite the Holy Spirit with the Power of God's Word

Beth Moore said:

In Jeremiah 23:29, God said, "Is not my word like fire . . . ?" As we draw from this parallel, relating something we can't quite understand to something we can, picture the Holy Spirit like a flammable substance within us. Because oil was often associated with anointing in the Word, many scholars believed oil symbolized the Holy Spirit. For the sake of our analogy, let's imagine the Holy Spirit as flammable oil within us. Now, imagine this oil flooding us completely as we seek and receive by faith the filling of God's Holy Spirit. Next imagine the torch of God's Word and combining it with the oil of the Holy Spirit. What is the result? The consuming fire of our God blazes within us, bringing supernatural energy, glorious activity, and pure, unadulterated power.[1]

Beth gives a formula: "The Spirit of truth + the Word of truth = internal combustion."[2]

Read God's Word, and the Holy Spirit will ignite and guide you.

Ask for Wisdom

If you are walking in a dark night, know that God's Word will illuminate your path. "Your word is a lamp for my feet, a light on my path" (Ps. 119:105).

However, you may also need to ask for wisdom so God will make your path "shin[e] ever brighter till the full light of day"

(Prov. 4:18). So if you need wisdom, say, "Dear Lord, instruct me," or "show me what is keeping me from my miracle."

When I recently prayed such a prayer, God showed me I had not forgiven myself for not praying for my daughter's safety prior to the car crash that so grievously injured her. I dealt with this false guilt by asking God to forgive me for not praying protection over my daughter prior to the crash, then asking God to forgive me for not forgiving myself. Finally, I asked God for his power to forgive myself.

Afterward, I felt free and happy that my former self-condemnation would not interfere with God's purposes for my life.

So why don't you take some time to pray, "Lord, show me what you want me to know. Show me what is keeping me from my miracle."

Then listen, read the Word, and do as God reveals.

We Are His Hands

Another way to live sold out for God is to recognize that we're his hands. Rebekah Binkley Montgomery explained this beautifully:

> I dreamed I was sitting alone in my garden of prayer, waiting, hoping Jesus would meet me there. And He did come! Excited, I stretched out my hands toward Him. He eagerly responded, reaching back to me.
>
> Then I saw them: His hands—powerful carpenter's hands, sensitive and skilled but horribly mangled. The nail holes weren't tidy like I always imagined but ragged, gaping wounds. I could literally see through His hands—bones, sinews, muscle, and destruction.
>
> "Oh Jesus! Your hands! They're ruined."
>
> He turned them over, examining them from backs to palms. "When I hung on the cross they supported the entire weight of my body," He explained. "Not to make you feel guilty, but the

most damage was done when I took on the sin of the world. Sin is heavy."

I frequently have cause to remember.

Gently, I took His hands in mine, and for a time, we sat in silence while I studied His once beautiful, now disfigured hands. I see His fingerprints and trace their whorls. I think: These hands created the world and did miracles. These hands healed the lame, blind, and crippled; fed 5,000. They reached for a drowning Peter. These hands washed disciples' dirty feet and then blessed the bread and wine. These hands willingly were nailed to the cross and yet they still reach out to me. These hands bear the scars of true love.

"I'm so sorry," said I. "Is there anything I can do to help Your hands heal?"

Then He took my hands in His. "Can I use your hands? Will you help me with the work that needs to be done?"

My hands shook convulsively as I held them out before Him. "Oh Lord, how can You use mine? My hands don't have Your skill or power. And besides, Lord, You know my problem."

Of course, He did know. A wasting disease had cost me much of the use of my right hand and I had limited use of my left. I was frustrated doing everyday tasks let alone anything for His kingdom. Was He going to do a miracle and heal my hand so I could work better for Him?

Knowing what I was thinking, He smiled. He had an even greater miracle in mind. Then He held up His scarred hands to remind me. "Trust Me. I do some of my best work with less-than-perfect hands."

So I do as He asks. I trust Him. And He does have work for me to do. Sometimes very simple things—coffee with a new friend, a phone call to someone grieving, a visit and piece of pie for a shut-in, a letter to a person in jail, etc.—just loving, personal touches from Jesus using my less-than-perfect hands.

Then, too, He uses my hands in ways that totally surprise me, such as to start a cancer center in Haiti (I'm still shaking my head over THAT one!). Or paint Bible story murals in a hospital (With my limitations I still can't figure out how they turned out so well!)—nothing less than miracles done with my less-than-perfect hands.

> *To be the hands of Jesus, his Spirit must live in us, leading us to desire what he desires.*

Often, in my garden of prayer, I ask Him, "How are Your hands today?" He holds them up for me to see. I see that even though they're wounded, His hands still have the healing touch.[3]

To be the hands of Jesus, his Spirit must live in us, leading us to desire what he desires (Rom. 8:5). Then we follow those Spirit-breathed desires into our destinies by simply doing the next thing God places before us (Prov. 20:24–30).

We don't even have to worry about failing because Psalm 37:23 says, "The LORD makes firm the steps of the one who delights in him; though he may stumble, he will not fall, for the LORD upholds him with his hand."

His precious, precious hands.

Miraculous Prayer

> *Dear Lord,*
>
> *I will follow you and, in the process, allow you to use my hands to reach the hurting, hungry, and lost. As I touch those you love, please send your miracles of provision, health, courage, faith, hope, and love.*
>
> *In Jesus's name, amen.*

$\mathcal{S}$cripture to Ponder

(Read aloud)

God is not unjust; he will not forget your work and the love you have shown him as you have helped his people and continue to help them.

Hebrews 6:10

To see Linda and the men from Set Free Church, go to www. NeedMiracleBook.com or turn to page 206 for a QR code.

11

The Next Step Principle

To this you were called, because Christ suffered for you, leaving you an example, that you should follow in his steps.

1 Peter 2:21

I don't know about you, but sometimes I don't hear God as clearly as I want. Sometimes I'm so busy looking for a sign like a flashing arrow that I miss the fact that God wants to guide me with his peace. As I've continued to discover, God's peace is a sign that never fails.

A couple of years ago, I sought God for a clear answer regarding a decision that had either a yes or a no choice. But I heard nothing. With a deadline looming that required action, I kindly informed God that I would take his lack of providing me with a clear no as a yes.

Though I felt agitated in my spirit, I took the yes step, a choice that soon proved to be a disaster.

How had I missed God's direction? I asked myself. Then I realized the problem wasn't God; it was me. I'd failed to follow God's peace. I should have realized that the agitation I felt in my spirit as I stepped out of God's will was actually the sign I was looking for.

How glad I am that when I stumbled on the trail, God held me by my hand and walked me to a place where I could make a U-turn. My mistake cost me pain, time, and money, but even so, God used it as a great lesson. I learned that sometimes God gives me a clear sign and other times he wants me to be mature enough to recognize and follow his peace. Please pray:

> *Dear Lord,*
> *Teach me how to follow your peace as you guide me into the*
> *destiny you have prepared for me since the beginning of time.*
> *In Jesus's name, amen.*

When God calls us to take the next step, there are a few prayer principles we need to understand. They include:

- hearing from God
- recognizing God's answers
- praying in faith
- letting go of control
- being obedient
- following God even when afraid

Hearing from God

I want to return to this topic because it's an area we must get right if we want to take the next step with God. But it may be that you already hear God more than you realize.

For example, a pastor told me he met a young man in a park who was angry with God. Pastor Jake, who knew no details of the man's upbringing, told the man, "I perceive your dad was a military man and that you have a lot of anger toward him. I want you to know God is not like your dad. God does not withhold his love until you perform."

I asked Pastor Jake how he'd known this stranger's father was a military man. "Was he wearing a T-shirt that said so?"

He answered, "It just seemed clear."

I'm thinking this was "clear" to Pastor Jake because the Holy Spirit who lives inside Pastor Jake made it clear.

Some Christians would call this phenomenon a "supernatural word of knowledge." Others would simply say, "God told me." However you describe it, when you receive insight from God, it may not seem supernatural as much as it seems *clear*. In my experience, these times of clarity are most often accompanied by feeling God's love for either me or the person with whom I'm speaking. In those moments, experiencing the sensation of God's love gives me the confidence to step up and speak out what the Holy Spirit is prompting me to do or say.

> *When you receive insight from God, it may not seem supernatural as much as it seems clear.*

For example, I was recently talking with a woman I'd just met when I felt God's great love for her. That sense of love gave me the boldness to speak an insight I perceived as we talked. "I feel you've come from the school of hard knocks and God is using what you've learned to help others. He sees what you are doing and is very pleased."

She responded, "Hard knocks? You couldn't have known this, but my former husband used to beat me. I now work with other abused women in a ministry I founded." She beamed. "God just used you to encourage me."

It was true, I hadn't known her story. So when I'd mentioned the school of hard knocks, I'd only spoken that which seemed clear. Yet, despite my ignorance of her personal life, God inspired my words to have a meaning deeper than I knew.

I'm guessing you've also had these moments of Holy Spirit clarity, whether you've recognized them or not. Pay attention and obey the Spirit's promptings to speak or act as he leads. Just be careful to speak and act in God's love instead of your own schemes.

Recognizing God's Answers

Many of us struggle to recognize God's answers to our prayers. I once talked with a woman who told me, "I asked God for a financial miracle so I would have enough money to move. But I didn't get my miracle; instead, I got my tax refund, which will cover my moving costs. So I told God, 'Never mind about the miracle. I got it covered.'"

I laughed. "Hello! God gave you your miracle *in* your tax refund."

My friend is not the only one who's made this mistake. Many of us discount God's miracles when they seem too ordinary. But if we don't learn to recognize them, then develop an attitude of gratitude, we might miss seeing more of his miracles on our behalf.

Praying in Faith

Many Christians are disillusioned with God because they've been taught to "name it and claim it." The problem is that whenever these dear ones don't get what they've named and claimed, they feel like God has rejected them. It's heartbreaking that droves of people have left the church because of their resulting disillusionment.

Let's see if we can get to the bottom of how to pray in faith. For starters, faith is the key element in praying for miracles. Matthew says:

> Early in the morning, as Jesus was on his way back to the city, he was hungry. Seeing a fig tree by the road, he went up to it but found nothing on it except leaves. Then he said to it, "May you never bear fruit again!" Immediately the tree withered.
>
> When the disciples saw this, they were amazed. "How did the fig tree wither so quickly?" they asked.
>
> Jesus replied, "Truly I tell you, if you have faith and do not doubt, not only can you do what was done to the fig tree, but also you can say to this mountain, 'Go, throw yourself into the sea,' and it will be done. If you believe, you will receive whatever you ask for in prayer." (21:18–22)

To me, this says we should have faith to tell all problems or obstacles that keep us from God's provision or purpose to wither or to get out of the way. Examples of such prayers could include, "Tumor wither!" or, "Mountain of debt, cast yourself into the sea."

But if you're like me, some of your prayers of faith haven't had the result you wanted. But if faith is believing God is able, then what exactly is our hang-up?

Perhaps it's that we struggle with the idea of whether God is willing to answer our prayers. His willingness is a topic I'll continue to address, but for now let me encourage you to continue seeking him with your whole heart, reading the Word, and praising him, for the deeper you go with God, the more you'll understand and pray in his will.

But what happens when we pray in God's will and don't get the miracle we seek?

That actually happened to Jesus's disciples. It seems they failed to cast a demon out of a child. Now, we know it was God's will to cast the demon out, because moments later Jesus cast the demon out himself. He scolded his disciples by telling them, "You don't have enough faith. . . . I tell you the truth, if you had faith even as small as a mustard seed, you could say to this mountain, 'Move from here to there,' and it would move. Nothing would be impossible" (Matt. 17:20 NLT).

Of course, we know Jesus's disciples had some level of faith, or they wouldn't have tried to cast out the demon in the first place. The problem was that they needed to build a deeper faith in order to get a better prayer result. But how does one build a deeper faith?

In Mark, Jesus further explained the disciples' failure to cast out a demon by saying, "This kind can come out by nothing but prayer and fasting" (9:29 NKJV).

So to build your faith, try continued prayer *and* fasting, as discussed previously. Continue to seek and praise God while you fast.

Letting Go of Control

When you've continued to pray in faith, you've fasted, but you're still not getting the breakthrough you hoped for, you'll have to discern if your prayer is:

- not God's timing

  The solution: You need to spend more time waiting on the Lord. Some prayers take years or even decades before you see the answers. Sometimes the answers do come, but not in your lifetime. But no matter the outcome, trust God anyway. He's got it covered.

• not God's leading

The solution: You need to get back in step with God. You can do that by asking the Holy Spirit to guide you. Pray for God's direction, and then follow his peace.

• not God's will

The solution: Would it be prudent for you to ask all that displeased you to wither or to be cast in the sea? Of course not. So it could be that some things you pray for are out of God's will. Ask God to give you his desire when you pray, and continue to say, "Your will be done," whenever you are seeking a miracle (Matt. 6:10).

So what is God's will? Let's do a comparative study:

God's Will	The Enemy's Plan
to bring life	to kill
to heal	to make sick
to restore	to destroy
to free	to imprison
to save souls	to deceive

You'd think a list like this would make God's will easy to spot. But not always. For example, if you were a roving reporter back in Jesus's day and had stuck a microphone in my face and asked me if it was God's will for Jesus to die on the cross, I might have looked at our "God's will" list and answered, "Nope. God's will is *life* not *death*. Therefore, Jesus's death could not be God's will."

However, I would have been wrong, for Jesus had to die before he could come back to life and give us eternal life. So as you can see, we may not always have the big picture of God's strategy—to bring life, to heal, to restore, to free, or to save souls—when it comes to some of our own difficult circumstances. Therefore, we must continue to trust God and let go of the control we "thought" we had as we pray through our situations.

The Christian life is like serving under a general who hasn't shared all of his strategic battle plans with us. Still, we must trust and obey orders we don't understand if we want to win the war.

No matter what happens, we know that what the enemy meant for evil God can turn into good. Plus, we know that the blood of Jesus combined with our faith and prayer can defeat all of the enemy's evil intentions. Satan is *not* stronger than God. He *cannot* win. In fact, he is more afraid of you than you are of him, especially when you pray in God's will in faith and in the power and authority of the name and blood of Jesus.

The biggest problem in winning the war may not be fighting the devil but fighting off our own selfish desires. When we are more in tune with our own selfish goals than with God's will, we may attempt to manipulate God to get our own way when what we really need to do, if we want the best miracle possible, is to let go. For example, consider the woman who picks out a handsome man at church and decides she wants to marry him. She doesn't bother to ask God his opinion or even to rely on the leading of the Holy Spirit to guide her. Instead, she goes right to prayer, insisting on her own way. "This man is mine, God. I claim him! And because I have faith that you'll give him to me to be my husband, you will have to do as I say."

God may give her what she wants. But that doesn't mean her answered prayer will bring happiness. We should heed Psalm 106:13–15, which says, "They soon forgot His works; they did not wait for His counsel, but lusted exceedingly in the wilderness, and tested God in the desert. And He gave them their request, but sent leanness into their soul" (NKJV).

The kind of prayer that bypasses God's counsel or direction has caused many a person to earnestly pray for a mistake.

As for the woman in my example, it would be better if she changed her prayer to, "Dear Lord, if it is your will, please let me marry this man. If it is not your will, I let go and ask you to please send me someone even better. If it is in fact your will for me to marry, then I have the faith to say to this mountain, 'Move over. God is bringing me the man of my dreams.'"

Being Obedient

Has God ever called you to humble yourself and obey? That's exactly what happened to Naaman. He was an army captain, and when he heard God could heal him of his leprosy, he hurried to Israel to seek God's prophet. However, Elisha opted out of the meeting and sent a message stating that if the captain washed in the Jordan River seven times, God would heal him of leprosy.

Naaman was insulted. How dare this prophet suggest he bathe in a muddy river? Besides, if this so-called prophet didn't respect him enough to heal him himself, then why should he follow his suggestion?

Naaman started to leave in a rage, but his servants told him, "If the prophet had told you to do something great, would you not have done it? How much more then, when he says to you, 'Wash, and be clean'?" (2 Kings 5:13 NKJV).

Naaman rethought his reaction, went to the Jordan, and took the plunge. It was on his seventh dip that God completely healed him.

God wants our obedience because it breaks the yoke of pride, and broken pride brings miracles.

Speaking of pride, did you know many Christians today are not healed because they have not confessed their sins and prayed for one another? If you don't believe me, read James 5:16: "Therefore confess your sins to each other and pray for each other so that you may be healed."

Why would God ask us to do something as embarrassing as telling our dirty secrets to another Christian? Well, what if the reason is this: Confession humbles us and breaks the spirit of pride so we can pray and be healed? If you are really serious about getting a miracle from God, confess your sins to a trusted believing friend, then pray for one another and watch how God moves on your behalf.

But beyond confessing your sins and praying for believers, is there something God told you to do that you've ignored? Then it's time to humble yourself and take this next step as God has revealed it to you. God may not be able to move on your behalf until you move into position.

Follow God Even When Afraid

Sometimes following God's peace will lead you to do something fearful. But follow God's peace through the fear.

This is exactly what Queen Esther did. Esther was the only one in the kingdom who had the ability to warn the king of a wrong that would result in the deaths of many. However, to approach the king without being summoned could, depending on the king's mood, be a death sentence. But as Esther's uncle told her, "For if you remain silent at this time, relief and deliverance for the Jews will arise from another place, but you and your father's family will perish. And who knows but that you have come to your royal position for such a time as this?" (Esth. 4:14).

Esther, though afraid, stepped out to warn the king. She followed God's peace into danger, saying, "If I perish, I perish" (Esth. 4:16).

But God not only protected Esther but also saved the lives of her family and her people.

What about you? What will you do if God calls you to do something that scares you?

First, consider you may be here for that very purpose. Then, like Esther, do the thing God has called you to do, even if you have to do it afraid. As long as you follow God's peace into the next step of your journey, you will step from one miracle to another.

Miraculous Prayer

Dear Lord,

Teach me how to have the faith I need to pray in your will so that I can receive mighty breakthroughs in my life. Give me the strength to obey your calling on my life, even if I'm afraid of what you've asked me to do. Thank you that you'll never call me to go against your Word. Thank you that I can trust you and you'll never leave me. Thank you that you're always with me. I'll take the next step with you, no matter what.

In Jesus's name, amen.

Scripture to Ponder

(Read aloud.)

> Guide my steps by your word,
>   so I will not be overcome by evil.
>   Psalm 119:133 NLT

See Linda's interview at www.NeedMiracleBook.com or turn to page 206 for a QR code.

12

The Intercession Factor

We always pray for you, and we give thanks to God, the Father
of our Lord Jesus Christ.

Colossians 1:3 NLT

I sometimes wonder who Heaven considers to be today's
"who's who" of the faithful. Would the list include the pastor
who leads a church of twenty thousand, the evangelist who led a
million people to Christ this year, or the young girl in a far land
who risked her very life to share the gospel with her neighbors?

I'm sure these are the kinds of people God would pick for
such a prestigious list. However, I'm thinking we've forgotten
someone who's very dear to God's heart. She's easy to miss.
When you do see her, you might see her frail body, though God
sees a mighty prayer warrior standing in the gap for others.
You might see a drab face lined with wrinkles, though God
sees the beauty of vibrant prayers of faith that push back the
darkness over ministries and loved ones. You might see feeble

knees, though God sees lovely knees that have worn a carpet bare through hours in prayer.

It may very well be that these faithful prayer warriors, the ones who have sacrificed their time to pray through great battles on behalf of others, are those whom God would most likely recognize as modern heroes of the faith.

Maybe one of these heroes has even prayed for you. Now it's your turn to pray it forward and intercede for someone else.

But what exactly is intercession? Is it convincing God he should listen to your thoughts on how to straighten out the mess a family member has made of his life? Is it guiding or directing God with your ideas to help him meet the needs of loved ones?

God knows, loves, and understands the needs of those you are praying for even more than you do.

Though it's not wrong to share your thoughts or ideas with God when praying for someone else, don't get too smug. God knows, loves, and understands the needs of those you are praying for even more than you do. I like how Philip Yancey puts it: "What I desire in the people I pray for, God desires all the more."[1]

So think of intercession like this: When you pray for a friend, you actually bring your friend into the presence of a loving God.

Imagine, if we could open our eyes to see into the supernatural, we might see we're actually in God's throne room, with our hand on our friend's shoulder, asking God, "Lord, would you please provide for my friend's needs?"

That's a lovely image and one I pulled right out of a New Testament story about four men who brought their paralyzed friend to Jesus.

Bless their hearts! These men had faith to believe the impossible—faith to believe Jesus could heal their injured friend. But despite their great faith, they ran into a wall. It seems there was such a crush of people in and around the house where Jesus was teaching that these men couldn't get their friend into the front door, much less find a way to ask Jesus for a miracle.

Despite the fact these men were blocked from reaching Jesus, they still found a way inside. They climbed to the top of the house, dug a hole in the thatch roof, and then lowered their friend to the feet of Jesus.

As you can imagine, their floating friend suddenly had Jesus's full attention. Jesus responded by forgiving the man's sins then commanding him to rise and walk into his healing.

But I have to ask: If it's a contest for Jesus's attention, how can we land our prayer requests at his feet? It might be easy for our tiny pleas to get lost in the clamor of millions of prayers rising simultaneously from around the world. How do we break through the din so our prayers can be heard?

What we need is a change in our perspective. Our human thinking limits us because we believe God can pay attention to only one person at a time. However, because God lives outside of time, he has the ability to hear our individual prayers and to focus on those prayers as though they were the only prayers in the world. In other words, whenever you pray a prayer for a friend, it's like you've plopped your friend at the feet of Jesus—to receive his full attention.

How to Pray

I love being still before the Lord and acknowledging his presence when I'm praying for someone else. As I bring my friend's situation and needs to Jesus, I try to go deeper still and ask, "Lord, help me to pray in your will. Guide me as I pray for needed miracles for my friend."

Then I wait, listen, and watch to see if God gives me any insight on how to pray.

Recently, as I prayed for a friend in ministry, I got an impression my friend was under a fierce attack, though I had no idea what had happened. I pressed, "Lord, how then should I pray for her?"

In my mind's eye, the Lord showed me my set free prayer. *Pray your warfare prayer over her.*

I did and instantly felt relieved.

A few days later, when I finally reached my friend, I learned she'd been in a terrible legal battle over the custody of her aging mother. When she heard what I'd prayed, she said, "Your warfare prayers stopped the battle, and Mom is now safe in my care. I can't tell you how much I appreciate your miraculous prayers on my behalf."

Praying in Love

If you've ever felt God's love ignite as you've prayed for someone else, you'll understand Romans 5:5, which says, "God's love has been poured out into our hearts through the Holy Spirit, who has been given to us."

As an example of how God's love moves as we pray, let me tell you what happened as I prayed for Janie. One evening, as we sat in her living room, Janie told me, "I've cried out to God time and again, yet it seems that when it comes to my life, tragedy continues to build on tragedy. It makes me feel God loves everyone but me."

Janie stopped speaking and winced as she put her hand on the small of her back, shifting uneasily.

"What's wrong?" I asked.

She frowned. "It's my back. It's killing me."

"Let's pray," I said, intending to mention only Janie's back pain to God as I prayed with her about her troubles. But as

176

I bowed my head, I felt an outpouring of love for Janie. The resulting words that formed in my mouth were much bolder than I'd intended. "Lord, Janie doesn't believe you love her. Help Janie to turn her eyes from her problems to you. Help her to see you *do* love her."

I placed my hand on her shoulder, and when I did, I felt another surge of God's love flow through me, and so my bold words continued. "Lord, prove to Janie you love her by healing her back and taking away her pain. I speak to the pain and tell it to leave in the authority and power of the name and blood of Jesus."

I have to admit, I was a little shocked by what I'd prayed and was filled with fear. *If God didn't heal Janie of her back pain, wouldn't she see my unanswered prayer as more proof that God was against her?*

I opened my eyes and saw Janie's eyebrows arch as she touched the small of her back again. "It's gone!" she said, amazed.

I stammered, "Your pain?"

"My back pain left as you prayed."

What a God moment. Not only was Janie's back healed, but her faith was also restored and she began to understand that God did love her, despite her circumstances.

Now, that's a miracle.

While I admit I took what appeared to be an awful risk, I will also confess I couldn't help myself. As soon as I touched Janie and felt God's love, there was no stopping the words tumbling out of my mouth as the Holy Spirit guided my prayer.

But my prayers for Janie didn't stop when God healed her back. We've continued to pray against the difficulties she faces, and we've continued to see miracles in those same circumstances. The battle continues. But now Janie has a secret weapon. She *knows* God loves her, and as a result, she knows she will be victorious.

Let me encourage you. When you pray for someone and begin to feel the flow of God's love as you pray, you are experiencing the presence and power of the Holy Spirit.

Relax into his presence and continue to pray until your words subside. You may be surprised at what you pray, but as long as you are praying in the flow of God's gracious love, you are allowing the Spirit to lead. These kinds of precious prayers most often result in miracles.

Don't pray crazy things just to challenge God. Pray instead in love as the power of his Holy Spirit leads you to pray.

A Real Treasure Hunt

As the Holy Spirit opens your eyes, you'll begin to see that the people God has put into your life are treasures tempting enough for the enemy to covet, steal, or even try to destroy.

I was recently at a prayer conference where we were instructed to go on a special treasure hunt, the kind of treasure hunt where we left the safety of the church building to pray for total strangers.

I have to admit that the idea of praying for a stranger, in public mind you, was a bit out of my comfort zone. But my dear friends Carole and Joy teamed with me and convinced me to strike out on an adventure.

We huddled together in Joy's car, where in earnest prayer we asked God to give us clues about whom we should pray.

Then we waited quietly before the Lord. As we did, I began to get a few sketchy images in my mind's eye.

Carole said, "Does anyone have any idea whom we're looking for?"

"I don't know," I said, "but as we were praying, I thought of a Taco Bell sign and the color red."

"You must be hungry," Joy teased.

178

I chuckled. "The reason that's funny is because I also feel the person we're to pray for *is* hungry."

The three of us sped toward a shopping district where we soon spied a Taco Bell. Joy pulled her car into the parking lot, and the three of us looked at one another. "What are we supposed to do?" I asked. "Go inside to see if anyone who is hungry is also wearing the color red?"

Joy laughed. "Maybe. Let's find out."

Joy and Carole marched in through the door, but I shuffled my feet. My stomach did flip-flops while I battled the urge to run.

But once we got inside, we saw that the restaurant was deserted, except for a young man in a red and black uniform standing at the counter. The three of us looked at one another. "What do we do?" I asked, sincerely believing the answer was, "RUN FOR YOUR LIFE!"

But there we still stood, frozen at the front door and staring at the Taco Bell employee, who asked, "May I help you?"

Carole gave me a little shove, and the three of us approached the counter. Joy was the brave one. "The three of us are on a treasure hunt," she said.

"What kind of treasure hunt?" the young man asked.

"Actually," Joy said, "we've found our treasure. The treasure is you."

At that point, I was sure the young man would think we were on the prowl.

"Me?" he asked with all sincerity. "How could I be your treasure?"

Joy boldly continued, "God sees you as his treasure, and we feel he's called us to pray for you today. May we?"

"Certainly," the young man said. "My name is Zack."

Just then, the bell above the front door chimed, and another customer, a man I didn't know, walked in and stared at us as we began to pray.

Now that we had an audience, I was certain we should bolt. However, I suddenly began to feel God's love for Zack. We prayed that Zack would know God, know God's love for him, and know God would provide for him.

I noted that the man, now waiting in line behind us, also had his head bowed, and I began to relax. When we finished our prayer, Joy asked Zack, "Do you have any pain or particular needs?"

"No, I feel fine, though I'm flat broke."

Joy opened her pocketbook and handed Zack a ten-dollar bill. "Not anymore," she said.

Zack was stunned and stared at the money in his hand before looking back at Joy. "You'd do that for me?"

> *What would happen if we lived each day as if we were on a treasure hunt with God?*

The man waiting in line said, "What have I been telling you, Zack? God really does love you. He really will provide for you."

I left the restaurant with goose bumps. God not only had led us to Zack but also had led a man who'd already been praying for Zack to walk into our prayer meeting.

As we got back into the car, I told Joy, "It was incredible that you gave Zack a ten-dollar bill."

Joy shrugged. "You were right. Zack was the one who was hungry. God sent us on a divine appointment to pray for him and to put a bit of jingle into his pocket, just to show him God cared."

That was an amazing experience, but I have to ask myself, *Why was I so afraid?* Shouldn't I be living my life in such a way that I'm always looking for opportunities to find God's treasure outside the church? Shouldn't I always watch to see whom God wants me to reach out to and pray for?

What would happen if we lived each day as if we were on a treasure hunt with God?

The Blessing Factor

I got a phone call from a woman who was upset because of a strange game her son Josh had played at a neighbor's house. He'd been instructed to fling a coin at the wall and was told that if the coin stuck, that meant he had God's favor. But if the coin fell to the floor, that meant he was out of God's favor. His mother told me, "Everyone's coin stuck to the wall except for Josh's. He's now afraid God doesn't love him and that he may even be cursed. What should we do?"

This game is dangerous for a couple of reasons:

1. Sometimes we live out what we believe about ourselves. I would hate for young Josh to live out the idea he was unloved and cursed by God.
2. This game actually curses those whose coins fall to the floor because I believe our words and agreements can give power to the enemy.

I like neither of these results and would recommend against playing the game. That said, the good news is we can pray against deceit, false assumptions, curses, and lies that come against our loved ones. As I told Josh's mom, "Ask God to break the lies or curses resulting from this game off your son in the power and authority of the name and blood of Jesus."

She was glad to know what to do, but I had one more recommendation for her. "It's time you and your husband blessed your son so he will know he is blessed and not cursed."

The book *The Blessing* by John Trent and Gary Smalley says, "A family blessing begins with meaningful touching. It continues with a spoken message of high value, a message that pictures a special future for the individual being blessed, and one that is based on the active commitment to see the blessing come to pass."[2]

A blessing for Josh might start with a hand resting on his shoulder and sound like this:

> Josh, we bless you and tell you you're very special to God. He loves you and will be with you all of your life. God has planned a special future for your life, one that not only will bless you but also will bring blessings to others. Go forth with the knowledge that God loves you and that you have found favor in him.

Ah! For every parent to give their child a blessing. But you might ask, "Are blessings in the Bible?"

Yes. In fact, the Lord told Moses, "Tell Aaron and his sons to bless the people of Israel with this special blessing: 'May the LORD bless you and protect you. May the LORD smile on you and be gracious to you. May the LORD show you his favor and give you his peace.'"

The Lord ended this instruction with this promise: "Whenever Aaron and his sons bless the people of Israel in my name, I myself will bless them" (Num. 6:22–27 NLT).

Even Jesus scolded his disciples when they tried to keep the little children from coming to him for a blessing. He said, "'Let the children come to me. Don't stop them! For the Kingdom of God belongs to those who are like these children. I tell you the truth, anyone who doesn't receive the Kingdom of God like a child will never enter it.' Then he took the children in his arms and placed his hands on their heads and blessed them" (Mark 10:14–16 NLT).

Not only do I love the idea of blessing our children, especially if we are seeking miracles on their behalf, but I also think it would be marvelous if we would bless all who are dear to us with a blessing based on the one the Lord instructed Moses to give his people:

> May the LORD bless you
>> and protect you.
> May the LORD smile on you
>> and be gracious to you.
> May the LORD show you his favor
>> and give you his peace.
>
> Num. 6:22–26

This is also my prayer for you.

Miraculous Prayer

Dear Lord,

I praise you that I can enter your gates with thanksgiving and your courts with praise. How I love and worship you. Thank you too that I can bring this dear one _____ *with me and lay them at your feet. Because this one is a treasure to you, you love them and already know about their dilemma. Lord, I too am concerned about their dilemma of*

_____ *.*

Lord, I ask that you'd [provide for, heal, help, bless] this dear one. Increase my love for _____ *as well as my wisdom on how to pray in your will regarding their difficulty.*

[Listen quietly before the Lord, then pray anything he reveals to you here.]

Also, in the name and authority and power of Jesus and his blood, I cancel any assignment of the enemy regarding this dear one and their dilemma.

I praise you, Lord. You care and are moving in _____'s life. I leave this dear one with you and thank you for the resulting miracles.

In Jesus's name, amen.

Scripture to Ponder

As for me, far be it from me that I should sin against the LORD by failing to pray for you.

1 Samuel 12:23

To see Linda's interview about praying for others, go to www. NeedMiracleBook.com or turn to page 206 for a QR code.

13

The Miracle of It All

Ask and it will be given to you; seek and you will find; knock and the door will be opened to you.

Luke 11:9

When you're gutsy enough to ask God for the impossible, you'll find miracles, along with occasional disappointments. When disappointments come:

- don't give up
- wait on God's timing
- trust God

Don't Give Up

Ron Kincade, in his book *Prayer Dare*, said, "If you are like most people, you give up on your prayers far too quickly. George

Müller, the English orphanage director who was known for his prayers, wrote:

> The great point is to never give up till the answer comes. I have been praying every day for 52 years for two men, sons of a friend of my youth. They are not converted yet, but they will be! The great fault of the children of God is that they do not continue in prayer. They do not go on praying; they do not persevere. If they desire anything for God's glory they should pray until they get it.[1]

Kincade continues, "One of these men became a Christian at Müller's funeral. The other, some years later. So Müller's prayers were not answered until after he died."[2]

We forget that God's time line in answering our prayer requests can extend even beyond our earthly lives.

Wait on God's Timing

I was driving down the freeway on my way to host a live TV show. As I started up a hill, the traffic squealed to a halt. I wasn't worried about the delay at first, but as the minutes began to tick down to the live broadcast, I began to pray, "Lord, send angels to move this traffic." Fifteen minutes later, the traffic hadn't moved an inch, and I prayed again, "Lord, I need your perfect timing to get me to the studio."

Five minutes later, I still sat as fire trucks and ambulances began to maneuver through the crowded lanes.

Surely the traffic will move now! Yet I sat for another five minutes in gridlock. Finally, I called the station. "Judy, tell Trish I'm stuck in traffic," I told the receptionist. "Trish may have to open the show."

"Don't worry," Judy reassured, "you'll get here in God's perfect timing."

The second I hung up, the traffic began to move. When I crested the hill, I saw a terrific wreck. Somehow an SUV had flipped onto its back. I watched as emergency personnel worked to extract people from the wreckage.

I began to call on Jesus on behalf of the victims as I passed by. Then the roadway opened up and I resumed my journey. Ten minutes later, I pulled into the station's parking lot with just enough time to shake hands with my guest and slide into the seat in front of the camera as it blinked to life.

As I look back, it's clear I was inconvenienced by the traffic. However, I'd missed being involved in that crash by only a half dozen or so cars. If it weren't for God's perfect timing, I could have missed the show, or even the rest of my life. Plus, I don't think it was a coincidence that I was in a position to pray for the accident victims. God's timing is perfect. He had me right where he wanted me.

> *God's timing is perfect.*

So if you feel as though your prayers are stuck in traffic, know that God is not late. He has reasons for where you currently are, reasons that will protect you, reasons to help you be a blessing to others.

Trust God

We need to trust God, even when we lose the fight. When King David's young son became ill, David fasted and bitterly sought the Lord to heal his child. But after praying for seven days, the child died anyway. The king's advisers were amazed that David accepted the death of the child, even saying, "I fasted and wept while the child was alive, for I said, 'Perhaps the Lord will be gracious to me and let the child live.' But why should I fast when he is dead? Can I bring him back again? I will go to him one day, but he cannot return to me" (2 Sam. 12:22–23 NLT).

This shows amazing faith. Though God did not answer David's prayer for healing for his son, David continued to walk with the Lord, knowing he would indeed be reunited with his son on the other side of eternity.

If you've done all and the answer is no, that doesn't mean God doesn't love you. It simply means he has another plan and he will see you through.

Sandi Patty writes in her book *Falling Forward*:

It's interesting how God brings us to a point of full surrender. Catherine Marshall, the author of *Christy* and other classic books, is known for having coined the term "the prayer of relinquishment." She learned of the power of surrender, or the prayer of "I give up," when she had done all she knew to do, exhausted all medical resources, and prayed all the prayers she knew to pray during a long illness. Finally, she simply prayed, "I'm tired of asking. I'm beaten, finished. God, you decide what you want for me the rest of my life." Tears flowed. She had no faith as she understood faith to mean (a sort of "trying really, really hard to believe" kind of faith).

To Catherine's surprise—after she prayed the prayer of surrender, or relinquishment, or "I give up to whatever you want," peace entered. God touched her deeply, and in her case, this surrender actually started her own physical healing.[3]

Catherine was healed when she gave God the reins of her dilemma, then trusted in his will no matter what. Sometimes our greatest miracles come when we surrender all, put our problem in God's hands, and determine to trust him no matter the cost.

ℳiraculous Prayer

Dear Lord,

I praise your holy name!

Because I am not giving up on you, I come to you, trusting in your perfect will and timing regarding my prayer request for

_____.

However, I surrender this request totally to you.

Thank you that I can praise you because you know about this situation and have heard my cry of _____.

Thank you that I do not have to pray frantic prayers, for I know that you have heard my cries. Therefore, I wait on you with confidence, trusting that you are working everything out for the good. Thank you that one way or another everything is going to be all right because you make all the difference.

In Jesus's name, amen.

Scripture to Ponder

(Read aloud.)

Don't be weary in prayer; keep at it; watch for God's answers and remember to be thankful when they come.

Colossians 4:2 TLB

Join Linda as she discusses the miracle of it all at www.Need MiracleBook.com or turn to page 206 for a QR code.

Conclusion

I promised you would experience a miracle if you read this book. You've experienced the miracle of drawing nearer to the Lord, learning how to trust him no matter what. You've shed hindrances to prayer, freed yourself from bitterness, and learned to pray for others. You know God loves you and are walking closer to him. You have begun to see your difficulties as seeds of miracles as you've learned to watch God flip your problems into blessings. Plus, you've learned how to pray the prayer of faith.

It is my hope you will see more answered prayer than ever. But even more than that, I hope you will experience the miracle of peace.

Yesterday, a family member called me repeatedly about a looming concern with a ticking deadline. I promised to pray, and I did. I even worked myself into a prayer frenzy. It was in that moment I heard the still, peaceful voice of God. "Why are you so frantic?" he asked me.

"Because I'm so worried!"

His still, small voice spoke again. "Everything is going to be all right."

Peace flooded my being, and I laughed. Of course everything was going to be all right. I had already brought my prayer concern to God, hadn't I?

God's whisper made me wonder how much more peace I would have if I always believed that after giving God my prayer concerns everything was going to be all right.

How would that belief change you?

Take a deep breath. God has heard your cries. He's moving on your behalf. So no matter what happens, God sees, hears, and is responding. The answer may not come the way you requested, but God is turning the situation into a miracle of eternal value. Relax. Everything *is* going to be all right.

For more, go to www.NeedMiracleBook.com or turn to page 206 for a QR code.

Readers' Guide

I'm delighted you took this journey with me. We experienced so much with the Lord and discovered so many miracles along the way.

Now I invite you, individually or with your study group, to work through the following questions. Also, consider viewing the chapter videos and helps as you reflect on each chapter. You can find these helps at www.NeedMiracleBook.com or turn to page 206 for a QR code. Also, if you are meeting in a group, always end your time together by praying for one another individually.

Chapter 1: Need a Miracle?

1. How did Jesus turn his own suffering on the cross into his greatest miracle? What does this miracle mean to us?
2. Is it possible to love God without having a relationship with him? Why is loving God without having a relationship with him a problem? Is this the first time you've prayed to correct this problem?

3. If prayer is simply talking to God, then list five topics you could bring to God in prayer.
4. Reread John 14:1. What would happen if you could take this Scripture passage to heart? Turn this Scripture passage into a prayer.
5. Reread O. Hallesby's quotation and discuss ways to linger in God's presence.
6. Look up John 14:4–7 and read the passage aloud. According to this, what is the major benefit for those who remain in Christ?
7. Read Psalm 89:15–16, found at the end of this chapter, aloud. Name three attributes this passage gives to people who walk in God's presence.
8. Share prayer requests and pray for one another.

Chapter 2: The Trust Factor

1. What are the benefits of troubles? Have you ever experienced a time when God met you in your trouble? Tell what happened.
2. Do you ever feel jealous when others seem to lead a trouble-free life? Pray for someone you may have felt jealous toward. Pray that they would find God or that when it's their turn to face trouble that God will bring them through it.
3. List the reasons it's okay to pray for miracles.
4. Review and discuss why God performs miracles today.
5. Why does God sometimes say no to our prayers?
6. Review the steps to help you prepare for a miracle. Pray the prayer that follows.
7. Read the paraphrased Psalm 91 together.

Chapter 3: The Love Factor

1. Why didn't Ron want to bring his aching back to God's attention? Was this a valid reason? Why or why not?
2. Look up and read aloud Psalm 139:17–18. How does this apply to you?
3. What was the lesson Nancy learned in the storm? Reread the Scripture passages that came to Nancy's mind when they were caught in the storm, then together pray Nancy's prayer.
4. How is Satan like an identity thief? Why is it so important to believe that God's love is for each of us?
5. Take a look at the list concerning who you are in Christ. Identify the attribute that is easiest for you to believe about yourself. Also identify the attribute that is most difficult for you to believe. Read the attribute's accompanying Scripture passage aloud, then paraphrase the passage as a prayer, asking God to give you the faith to believe this attribute about yourself.
6. Pray the miraculous prayer out loud with your group.
7. Read John 14:18 aloud. What does this verse mean to you?

Chapter 4: The Truth Factor

1. It stands to reason that if a computer program has a creator, so must we. What is the divine truth of why God created each of us?
2. Look up and read John 16:13–16. According to this, what does the Holy Spirit, or Spirit of truth, do for us?
3. Discuss why it's important to read God's Word. Strategize how you could read God's Word daily. Share your plan with the group.

4. What difference did it make in Linda's life to pray Ephesians 6:13–17 daily? What difference do you think such a prayer could make in your life? Turn Ephesians 6:13–17 into a prayer of your own.

5. Who are some biblical greats who prayed for God's will? Discuss the reasons why it is important that we pray in God's will.

6. Discuss the story of the woman in Matthew 9:20–22. Why do you think God healed this woman? How does her story relate to how we should pray?

7. In the section "Is God's Will Always No?" Linda tells how God healed her emotional pain and Carole's physical pain. Do you think it could be God's will to heal you this way as well? Why or why not? Pray the prayer included in this section for yourself and others in the group.

Chapter 5: The Forgiveness Factor

1. Why is it important to God that we forgive others? What price did God have to pay to forgive us?

2. Go back and reread the list of benefits of forgiveness. Follow that by reading the Dwight L. Moody quotation just below the list. Why would these benefits be important to you?

3. According to Everett Worthington, what are some of the health risks associated with unforgiveness? What are some additional disadvantages of unforgiveness according to Denise George and Corrie ten Boom? Discuss why developing a forgiving heart might help correct these problems and conditions.

4. Think of Rosemary Trible's story and discuss how forgiveness can change eternity. Why would this be a good thing?

5. What was causing Linda's barrier with God? As a group, pray the prayer together that Linda prayed.
6. Who were the three people Linda led Darla to forgive? Why? How was it possible for Darla to forgive? What were the benefits to Darla?
7. Think of the story about the military wives who were having difficulty forgiving others. What helped them forgive?
8. Pray the miraculous prayer at the end of the chapter together.

Chapter 6: What Hinders Our Prayers?

1. Read through the hindrance list and put a check by the hindrances that have troubled you the most. Select a hindrance and tell the group how you are working or will work to correct it.
2. Look up the Scripture passages in the list found in "Wrong Perspectives of God" and discuss how they relate to the truths listed in this section.
3. In Mark 9:21–27, why do you think Jesus healed the boy despite his father's apparent lapse of faith? What should we do when we receive a bad report?
4. Why didn't the disciples recognize Jesus? Why and how should we avoid focusing on our disappointments?
5. Why did God punish the Israelites who complained in the desert? Why is it important for us to praise instead of grumble?
6. Reread the quotations from Richard J. Foster and discuss why it's good that God doesn't always answer our prayers the way we want.
7. Have each person pick out their favorite prayer in the chapter and lead the group to pray it together.

Chapter 7: Fighting the Enemy

1. Read Matthew 6:13 and John 10:10. Then explain whether, according to Jesus, we should learn how to pray against our enemy, Satan.
2. Many believe that because the devil is *not* hiding behind every bush, we should not worry about the impact of evil in our lives. Read Ephesians 6:12–13 and 2 Corinthians 10:3–5. Then explain how you would answer this criticism.
3. Why should we pray in the authority and power of the blood and name of Jesus?
4. Using the prayer Linda led the pastors' wives to pray, pray it for your church and/or the churches in your community.
5. Why is it more important to focus on God than to focus on evil or the enemy? Do we need to be afraid of the enemy?
6. Together, pray through the entire set free prayer. Then talk about what it means to you.

Chapter 8: More Strategies for Fighting the Enemy

1. Reread 1 Peter 5:8–9. What would make someone an easy target for the schemes of the enemy? Why do we need to stay alert?
2. How would you instruct someone to pray who has received a negative message from the enemy? Write the prayer to combat negative messages and then pray it together.
3. Why is it important not to parrot negative messages about yourself or others? What should you do if you have been guilty of this?
4. If you haven't already, follow Linda's example to bless your home. If you are with a group, take turns praying a blessing over each home represented.

5. Discuss what C. S. Lewis said about soul connections. What's the best way to break these unwanted connections from the past?
6. Read both the prayer and the Scripture passage at the end of the chapter aloud.
7. Spend some time praying for one another's needs.

Chapter 9: The Praise Factor

1. Reread Psalm 22:3 and describe what you think it means.
2. What are the four things that praise helps us accomplish?
3. Look up Psalm 40:1–5. Read it as a prayer of praise unto God.
4. How does praise help us win the battle? Each person should take a moment to pick a problem, then one by one, like David did with Goliath, introduce the problem to God.
5. Do you think praise was a factor in Linda's brother's healing? Why or why not?
6. Reread Beth Moore's quotations near the end of the chapter. Do you think she got it right? Why or why not?
7. Go back through the chapter and pray each prayer together.

Chapter 10: The Sold Out Factor

1. What are the four things we need to do if we want to live sold out lives?
2. Discuss Jeremiah 10:23. How would it look to live this Scripture? How would living this Scripture change your life?
3. If the Holy Spirit dwells in our bodies, how should that affect the way we live?

4. Pray the prayer found in the section "Understand That the Holy Spirit Dwells in Us." Then discuss how it will impact your life.
5. Describe how Beth Moore explains how the Word ignites the Holy Spirit inside of us.
6. Reread Rebekah Montgomery's story about the hands of Jesus. How would your life change if you allowed Jesus to use your hands as his hands? What would he call you to do that you are not already doing? Spend a moment asking God to help you be his hands.
7. Read the miraculous prayer and Scripture to ponder aloud together.

Chapter 11: The Next Step Principle

1. What should you follow as a sign of God's direction?
2. What are the prayer principles we need to follow if we want to live the next step principle?
3. Sometimes God's direction doesn't seem supernatural; it seems _____ (fill in the blank). Give a personal example, if you can, as to what this means.
4. What mistake did the woman with the tax refund make? Why do many of us discount God's miracles? What should we do about this problem?
5. According to Mark 9:29, what did Jesus tell his disciples about how to build a deeper faith? If you've done this and you're still not getting your breakthrough, what are three things that could be the reason? What are the solutions?
6. Based on Psalm 106:13–15, what might be a better way to pray?
7. Read James 5:16, and, following its advice, spend time confessing to and praying for one another. For example, say something like, "I would like to be a better person and

stop _____. I'm telling you so you can hold me accountable and pray for me." After each confession, pray for the one confessing. Pray they can overcome, and pray for any special prayer need they have as well. Be careful what you confess to mixed groups of men and women. You may need to divide into groups of the same sex to do this exercise. Also, note that confidentiality is required. Be careful what you confess to someone who confesses to being a gossip.

Chapter 12: The Intercession Factor

1. Look up and read Luke 11:9. How do you apply these words of Jesus to your life?
2. Using Linda's model of bringing friends or family members into the presence of God, spend time praying for your various loved ones. This is your opportunity to do some important prayer work.
3. If a member of your group has a pain, health, or other issue, spend some time praying for them. With their permission, touch their head, hand, arm, or shoulder. Then let the Holy Spirit guide your words with his love.
4. Take the time to pray the blessing at the end of chapter 12 over every member of your group. With their permission, touch their hand, head, arm, or shoulder as you pray.
5. Make a date to go on a treasure hunt to pray for strangers outside the church using the model Linda writes about. Discuss when and where you could meet. If you have the time now, why not get started? (See webpage for more instructions on how to do a treasure hunt.)

Chapter 13: The Miracle of It All

1. What are three things you can do when you face disappointments? Why?
2. Like Catherine Marshall, write a prayer of surrender concerning your difficulties and offer it to God.
3. Spend some time praising God that everything is going to be all right.
4. On one hand, Linda says, "Never give up," but at the same time she says, "Pray the prayer of relinquishment." What is the difference between the two ideas? Which idea do you need to work on and why?
5. Make a list of miracles you received while reading this book. Share them with the group.
6. Go around the group, each thanking God for the miracles/blessings received.
7. Read the miraculous prayer together.
8. Turn the Scripture to ponder into a prayer and say it together.
9. Take time for prayer requests and pray for one another.

Notes

Chapter 1: Need a Miracle?

1. Sarah Young, *Jesus Calling: Enjoying Peace in His Presence* (Nashville: Thomas Nelson, 2004), 51.

2. Andrew Murray, www.famousquotesandauthors.com.

3. *The Book of Positive Quotations*, 2nd ed., compiled and arranged by John Cook, edited by Steve Deger and Leslie Ann Gibson (Minneapolis: Rubicon, 1996), 189.

Chapter 2: The Trust Factor

1. Philip D. Yancey, *Prayer: Does It Make Any Difference?* (Grand Rapids: Zondervan, 2006), 260.

2. Linda Evans Shepherd, *When You Can't Find God: How to Ignite the Power of His Presence* (Grand Rapids: Revell, 2011), 145–46.

3. Peggy Joyce Ruth, *Psalm 91: God's Shield of Protection* (Lake Mary, FL: Charisma House, 2007), 129.

Chapter 3: The Love Factor

1. Sue Cameron, *Teatime Stories for Women*, compiled by Linda Evans Shepherd (Tulsa: Honor Books, 2000), 10–12.

2. Nancy Bayless, *Heart-Stirring Stories of Love*, compiled by Linda Evans Shepherd (Nashville: Broadman & Holman, 2000), 56.

3. Stormie Omartian, *The Prayer That Changes Everything: The Hidden Power of Praising God* (Eugene, OR: Harvest House, 2004), 54.

Chapter 4: The Truth Factor

1. Debbie Alsdorf, *A Different Kind of Wild: Is Your Faith Too Tame?* (Grand Rapids: Revell, 2009), 55.

2. *The Book of Positive Quotations*, 2nd ed., compiled and arranged by John Cook, edited by Steve Deger and Leslie Ann Gibson (Minneapolis: Rubicon, 1996), 196.

Chapter 5: The Forgiveness Factor

1. *The Book of Positive Quotations*, 2nd ed., compiled and arranged by John Cook, edited by Steve Deger and Leslie Ann Gibson (Minneapolis: Rubicon, 1996), 199.

2. Stephen Stevens, *The Wounded Warrior: A Survival Guide for When You're Beat Up, Burned Out* (Sisters, OR: Multnomah, 2006), 54.

3. Quote from Everett Worthington in Denise George, *Cultivating a Forgiving Heart: Forgiveness Frees Us to Flourish* (Grand Rapids: Zondervan, 2004), 76.

4. George, *Cultivating a Forgiving Heart*, 80.

5. Ibid.

6. Francis Bacon, *Quotes about Forgiveness*, www.QuotationsBook.com.

7. Corrie ten Boom, *Tramp for the Lord* (New York: Penguin Group, 1982), 55.

8. Rosemary Trible, *Fear to Freedom: What If You Did Not Have to Be So Afraid?* (Sisters, OR: VMI, 2009), 103.

9. Henry Wadsworth Longfellow, *Quotes about Forgiveness*, www.QuotationsBook.com.

10. Ten Boom, *Tramp for the Lord*, 10.

11. *Barnes' Notes Electronic Database Biblesoft*, 1997.

Chapter 6: What Hinders Our Prayers?

1. Charles F. Stanley, *Discovering Your Identity in Christ* (Nashville: Thomas Nelson, 1999), introduction.

2. *The Book of Positive Quotations*, 2nd ed., compiled and arranged by John Cook, edited by Steve Deger and Leslie Ann Gibson (Minneapolis: Rubicon, 1996), 192.

3. Ibid.

4. Elmer L. Towns, *The Beginners' Guide to Fasting* (Ventura, CA: Gospel Light, 2009), 11.

5. Kenneth Boa, *Conformed to His Image: Biblical and Practical Approaches to Spiritual Formation* (Grand Rapids: Zondervan, 2001), 246–47.

6. Ibid., 247.

7. Richard J. Foster, *Finding the Heart's True Home* (San Francisco: Harper-Collins, 1992), 182.

8. Ibid., 183.

9. Cited in ibid., 182.

Chapter 8: More Strategies for Fighting the Enemy

1. Charles F. Stanley, *When the Enemy Strikes: The Keys to Winning Your Spiritual Battles* (Nashville: Thomas Nelson, 2006), 6.

2. C. S. Lewis, *The Screwtape Letters* (San Francisco: HarperCollins, 2001), 95–96.

3. Ibid., 96.
4. Linda Evans Shepherd, *Tangled Heart: A Mystery Devotional* (Longmont, CO: Jubilant, 2006), 235–36.
5. Ibid., 236.

Chapter 9: The Praise Factor

1. Biblesoft's New Exhaustive Strong's Numbers and Concordance with Expanded Greek Hebrew Dictionary (Biblesoft & International Bible Translators, 1994).
2. Stormie Omartian, *The Prayer That Changes Everything: The Hidden Power of Praising God* (Eugene, OR: Harvest House, 2004), 252.
3. Ibid.
4. David Jeremiah, *My Heart's Desire: Living Every Moment in the Wonder of Worship* (Nashville: Thomas Nelson, 2004), 130.
5. Beth Moore, *Breaking Free: Making Liberty in Christ a Reality in Life* (Nashville: Broadman & Holman, 2000), 58.
6. Ibid.

Chapter 10: The Sold Out Factor

1. Beth Moore, *Believing God* (Nashville: Broadman & Holman, 2004), 130.
2. Ibid.
3. Rebekah Binkley Montgomery, *His Scars* (Longmont, CO: Right to the Heart of Women Ezine, 4/6/11).

Chapter 12: The Intercession Factor

1. Philip D. Yancey, *Prayer: Does It Make Any Difference?* (Grand Rapids: Zondervan, 2006), 303.
2. John Trent and Gary Smalley, *The Blessing* (Nashville: Thomas Nelson, 1993), 25.

Chapter 13: The Miracle of It All

1. Ron Kincade, *Prayer Dare: Take the Challenge That Will Transform Your Relationship with God* (Ventura, CA: Regal Books, 2010), 38.
2. Ibid.
3. Sandi Patty, *Falling Forward: Into His Arms of Grace* (Nashville: Thomas Nelson, 2007), 151.

LINDA EVANS SHEPHERD is the author of over thirty books, including *When You Can't Find God: How to Ignite the Power of His Presence* and *When You Don't Know What to Pray: How to Talk to God about Anything*, as well as the bestselling novel series the Potluck Club and the Potluck Catering Club, written with Eva Marie Everson.

An internationally recognized speaker, Linda has spoken in almost every state in the country and around the world. You can learn more about her speaking ministry at www.Linda EvansShepherd.com.

Linda is the president of Right to the Heart Ministries. She is the CEO of AWSA (Advanced Writers and Speakers Association), which ministers to Christian authors and speakers. To learn more about Linda's ministries, go to www.VisitLinda.com.

Linda has been married to Paul for over thirty years and is the mother of two children.

To find more information about this or other books by Linda, go to www.NeedMiracleBook.com or use the QR code below:

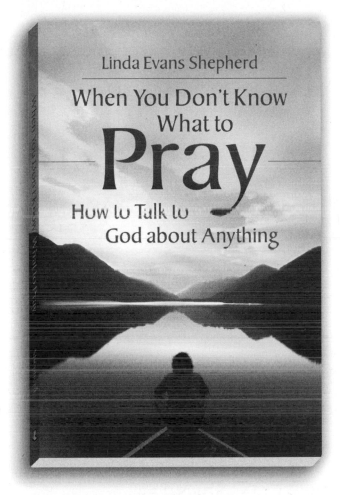

You *can* find hope and peace— no matter what.

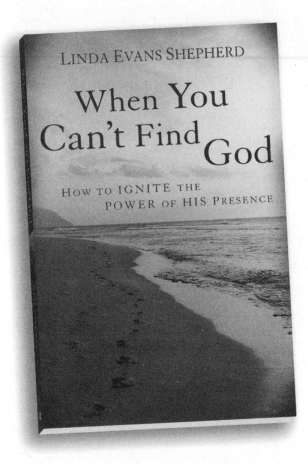

LINDA EVANS SHEPHERD teaches you how to see God in any circumstance, even when it's hard.

Visit www.ignitemyfaith.com to learn more.